Digging the Dirt with
Time Team

Digging the Dirt with
Time Team

TIM TAYLOR

Photographs by Chris Bennett

First published in 2001 by Channel 4 Books, an imprint of Pan Macmillan Ltd,
Pan Macmillan, 20 New Wharf Road, London N1 9RR, Basingstoke and Oxford.

Associated companies throughout the world

www.panmacmillan.com

ISBN 0 7522 6161 4

9 8 7 6 5 4 3 2 1

A CIP catalogue record for this book is available from the British Library.

Drawings by Victor Ambrus
Design by designsection, Frome, Somerset
Colour reproduction by Aylesbury Studios
Printed and bound in Great Britain by Bath Press

All photographs were shot using Nikon F5 cameras, fitted with Nikkor lenses ranging from 16mm to 300mm,
and on Kodak Elitechrome Extra Colour transparency film. Processing by Ceta of Poland Street, London.

This book accompanies the television series *Time Team* made by Videotext Communications in association
with Picture House Television for Channel 4.
Executive producer: Philip Clarke
Producer: Tim Taylor

Contents

INTRODUCTION: THE RESEARCH CRISIS

We always begin the research process with a lot of great potential sites but, as the date for finalising the first eight or ten locations out of the thirteen *Time Team* visits each year draws nearer, our questions become more rigorous. Each possible site has to be forced through the filter of whether it will make good television. Is there a story that will carry us through – an idea that viewers can hold in their heads through the various circuitous routes the archaeology will take?

At the start of 2001 we had some classic and typical problems with the sites for Series Nine. It was as if we were alchemists trying to make gold from base metals – each location seemed to be a bundle of floating possibilities and needed something radical to turn it into reality. It almost felt as though we should hit the sites hard to see if they would stand up and turn into solid reality.

The programme we had begun to call the 'bronze bucket show' needed careful political handling as conflicting archaeological interests were connected with it. A site in Tara, with a set of geophysics results that John Gater described as 'stonking', was hanging in the air because our Irish archaeological contact had not yet been appointed as official contractor. A site at Vauxhall on the Thames seemed likely to be overwhelmed by rising tidal levels that were threatening to turn it into a dive site. A number of other possible sites were held up by warring landowners, illegal metal detecting and, in one case, the likelihood that digging behind a pub might make the walls collapse.

On 9 February the first major meeting with the directors was only twelve days away and soon after that the production team would have to start booking hotels, flights, etc. But too many sites were still in what you might call the 'float' mode. At this point, as always, the researchers and I shared a range of sensations and feelings. We all had a desperate need for what one of them called 'closure' on the sites, yet we had to be sure that the choices we made were the right ones before presenting them to the directors and Channel 4.

The previous year had started with a 'whimper' not a bang, and I did not want this to happen again. The shoot by the railway line at Basildon, Berkshire was supposed to find a Roman villa but it didn't and it's always a bit of a disappointment when the first programme of the year fails to hit its target. In the end they were all good viewing but the year began with a degree of uncertainty that was only really dispelled by the heroic job the whole team did at Blaenavon in south Wales in the third programme in the series.

I have to wear two hats at this stage of the research process – one of which might be called my 'telly' hat. This requires a hard-nosed approach to a site, which will either push it into closure or reject it. Some researchers are better at 'closure' than others because they get less involved in the archaeology and don't take it too personally when a favourite site has to be abandoned. There is a distinct difference between a good story and good archaeology. The latter may involve a site that is worth excavating from an archaeological point of view but has nothing that will grab either the team or the viewer. At this stage I like to get Phil Clarke's and Tony's point of view. As the executive producer, Phil brings a pragmatic and non-archaeological perspective to the potential choice of sites and Tony has a gut feel for the kind of ideas the viewers will like most.

From the first block of ten to twelve ideas, I liked the idea of excavating on the banks of the Thames because it was a massive challenge – the tides meant we would only have two hours a day to dig – and it was also fascinating to think that Bronze Age posts were sticking out of the water. The idea of fantastic Roman archaeology under a supermarket car park in Castleford in West Yorkshire seemed good, and the potential of a large lump of industrial archaeology under a pub in Leighton in Shropshire had a nice quirky ring about it.

Other sites seemed potentially exciting, but needed more archaeological information. For example, we had a great 'allotment site' which had a lot of good finds, but it lacked a clear archaeological goal. Sites are often abandoned for this reason. Archaeologists are not used to giving their views quickly. Decisions and ideas are checked out over months and years, so it is difficult for our researchers to ask them to get a move on – and too much pressure to firm up a site can backfire.

The idea of a dive to search for a Spanish galleon in the far north of Scotland sounded fantastic, but would need a great deal of research as we would be committing a lot of money and effort. Shoots like this are notoriously uncertain due to the British weather and because visibility can be poor underwater.

Yet other sites seemed a bit bland and lacked exciting goals. I was unconvinced about a manor house. So we find it – who cares? Our potentially wonderful allotment site – artefacts among the cabbages – which was being vigorously supported by a local amateur archaeologist still lacked a key archaeological focus at its core. It had a wonderful connection with the diarist John Evelyn, and tons of flint and pottery, but both Jenni Butterworth and I felt it didn't have a basic structure that we could pursue.

At this stage I have to be careful to distinguish between a side of me that is interested in a whole range of archaeological work and wants to support local initiatives, and the side that knows we only have thirteen slots a year – and that each site has to fight to get in. I have to back my hunches and go for the sites I believe will work for *Time Team*.

We were also looking at the general mix of period, location and subject to make sure that the balance of the series would be right. For example, I always feel that once we have two or three good Roman sites we need ones from other periods to counterbalance them. And I am always looking for archaeology in places where you wouldn't expect it – sites that lift the series because of their unusual or quirky nature. In previous series the Spitfire shoot in France, and those in Blaenavon and the backstreets of Soho in Birmingham all had this quality.

Finally, we always have to be aware of Channel 4's reaction to previous programmes. This can make it difficult to get some sites past the commissioning editor. For example, there was a feeling that prehistoric programmes didn't 'work' – and therefore a reluctance to consider sites from this period.

By the end of February the list of potential locations had been narrowed down to a shortlist of twenty and Jenni was checking how many of them were scheduled sites for which SAM (Scheduled Ancient Monument) applications would have to be written. SAMs are protected by the government and need the Secretary of State to give approval for excavation to take place. An application has to be made that includes a rigorous research design detailing our exact plans, listing who will be involved and addressing the reasons why we believe the site should be excavated. Even then it is far from certain that permission will be granted.

Jenni and I had had an excellent meeting with English Heritage at the start of the year and were able to discuss ideas for the approaches to archaeology that they would like to see being addressed in the programmes. We had also been able to tell them about the progress of reports on previous sites. I was delighted to be able to show that 80 per cent of our sites have been written up or are part of a larger report – a record comparable to that of many professional units. We have appointed another archaeologist Kate Edwards whose job will be purely to record and write-up our sites.

Jenni was, I think, relieved that she could begin writing research designs for our shortlisted sites and worry less about which locations might finally make it.

It seemed, however, that one last push had to be made. Too many sites were still in 'float' mode. We cancelled meetings and everyone in the development team concentrated on CLOSURE! The tension was making us jumpy, and the rest of the production team wanted to ask where they would be working over the next few months – but, for most of the time, they showed admirable restraint.

The pressure of the approaching deadline meant tough decisions had to be made. In a series of tense meetings some sites were abandoned and others committed to. Phone calls were made to saddened local archaeologists and anxious questions asked about the weather in Scotland. By February I was at a point where I could send an initial list to Channel 4. It would interesting to see which ones would make it through to filming.

It was also at this stage that we divided up the potential sites between the teams. Our new assistant producer, Sarah Walmsley, would oversee the research team, with our other long-serving assistant producer, Ella Galinski, taking care of the cameos. The two researchers, George Pagliero and Ishbel Macdonald, would work on half the programmes each, with the junior researcher, Ben Dempsey, mopping up any extra as needed.

We still had a number of worries including high tides, torrential rain and its effect on river levels, discontented local farmers facing falling milk prices and the threat to a couple of our sites by some unscrupulous metal detectors. It was the usual challenging start to the year. Jenni and I were getting to the 'worried' stage and I had begun to have the odd sleepless night. Channel 4 had our list and we had made a commitment. We had some reserve sites in hand, but this is always a nerve-racking moment. The first meeting with the directors was scheduled for 21 February when we would tell them which sites they would be filming.

It was during this week that foot-and-mouth disease was confirmed on a small farm in Essex. Of our potential twenty sites, twelve were on or near farms. We now had just two or three weeks to reorganise the first twelve shoots and replace farm sites with those near industrial areas, towns or anywhere not occupied by or adjacent to a cow or sheep. It's surprising how difficult this is to do in Britain. Apparently urban sites suddenly turned out to have small pockets of valuable livestock in them and the general paranoia that the disease was creating meant the last thing landowners wanted was a film crew traipsing over their land. It would mean that our first few sites could not include the ones we had banked on. This was to prove an exciting, challenging and worrying start to Series Nine.

The Thames is a major route into the heart of England and has carried shipping since the prehistoric period. Consequently it contains landmarks from many historic periods. What an earth will future archaeologists make of Battersea Power Station?

VAUXHALL
London

'THIS IS A RACE AGAINST TIME LIKE NEVER BEFORE'

Tony Robinson's piece to camera: 'Welcome to the banks of the Thames at Vauxhall in central London. It's seven o'clock in the morning and in less than an hour's time a mysterious structure – a series of 3,500-year-old wooden posts – will begin to emerge from the receding waters. Could these Bronze Age remains be part of a building? Maybe they supported a pier from which beautiful votive objects, like this spearhead [holds up spearhead], were offered to the Thames. Or perhaps they're just all that remains of London's first bridge. As usual *Time Team* have got just three days – but because we are dealing with tidal waters, we can only get at this structure for two hours a day. So can we solve this mystery in just six hours digging? This is a race against time like never before.'

The Bronze Age

It is rather ironic that the Bronze Age, a period that archaeologists defined by using the name of a metal, could be characterised just as effectively by the extraordinary expertise in the use of timber shown by the people of the time. *Time Team* has helped to demonstrate this clearly enough through its involvement in the excavation of remarkable wooden structures from this period at Greylake on the Somerset Levels (dating to about 900 BC), and at Flag Fen in Cambridgeshire. And in the heart of London, on the Thames foreshore at Vauxhall, the discovery of twenty-seven robust, load-bearing timbers may mark the site of a bridge built in the Bronze Age, the earliest so far known.

Not only did the use of wood as a construction material continue, and indeed expand, in the Bronze Age, but flint continued to be extensively used throughout the period – and far outweighed bronze for the manufacture of tools for everyday use. None the less, the introduction of the first metal tools to Britain, probably shortly after 2,500 BC and from sources in Ireland, marks a defining moment in British prehistory. Those early tools were made from arsenical copper; bronze itself, an alloy of tin and copper, seems to have made its appearance in Britain by about 2,000 BC.

In fact, the early Bronze Age (about 2,000 to 1,600 BC) was in many ways a continuation of the preceding Neolithic period. People continued to build large funerary and ritual monuments, such as barrows and stone circles, just as they had done before – these were landscapes of the dead. From the middle of the Bronze Age onwards, however, the emphasis changes and we begin to see far more concern with dividing up the landscape. As one expert has put it, the landscapes of this period were very much landscapes of the living. The greater strain on resources brought about by a growing population may have made control over land, and the demarcation of boundaries, the most critical concerns of the rulers of late Bronze Age society.

One of the principal differences between the Bronze Age and the earlier period seems to have been a move away from the use of the monuments known as long barrows, which were used to deposit the remains of numerous individuals, and the appearance instead of smaller mounds, of which the well-

known round barrow is the most common. Until quite recently archaeologists saw these smaller mounds as representing a complete change from the communal burials of the long barrows to a far more individualistic type of interment under round barrows – they supposedly contained the remains of elite members of the community while 'ordinary' people were more likely to be cremated. However, we know now that many Bronze Age barrows were used for multiple burials. The difference from the Neolithic long barrows seems to be that often each burial was inserted into the barrow separately, and each was accompanied by its own set of grave goods.

Both individual barrows and entire barrow cemeteries could be placed very close to houses – so the dead were very much a part of the everyday world of the living. Indeed, it seems as though in some cases, as at Brenig in north Wales, funerary monuments were built directly over former dwellings, and it may be possible, as the eminent prehistorian Professor Richard Bradley of Reading University has suggested, to see 'the great barrow cemeteries … as the settlements of the dead'.

Previous page: Early morning by the river at Vauxhall. The bank in the foreground at high tide becomes covered with over 10 metres (33 feet) of water.

Above: From the London Eye, Mick and Stewart could take an overview of the site.

As we stood by the Thames at 7.15 in the morning I reminded myself why we had decided to do this site. I had liked its unexpected elements – who would expect a set of rather unimposing timbers to turn out to be Bronze Age? The area had also yielded two amazing bronze spearheads, which were some of the most beautiful objects we'd seen on *Time Team*.

The site – near Thorney Island below Vauxhall Bridge, in front of the MI6 building – had first been discovered in 1993 by a 'mudlarker'. These are people who have for many years scanned the edge of the Thames for objects of historical interest. They have a fairly secretive attitude to their work, but co-operate with the Museum of London when something of real interest turns up. Since the discovery, twenty-seven timbers had been recorded and there was a chance that there were many more that would be destroyed by river traffic. Some of them had been radiocarbon dated, producing a date of around 1,500 BC, yet very little evidence of what they had been used for had come to light.

Time Team were invited to investigate the site by the Museum of London and Gustav Milne, an expert on the Thames from the Institute of Archaeology. The site was possibly under threat from erosion and our close contacts with the museum through Hedley Swain, and with Gustav, led to them telling us about the discovery. For some time I had been looking for a site where we could investigate inter-tidal archaeology, and this one posed exactly the kind of unusual challenge that works for *Time Team*. Working on the site would also give us a chance to meet up again with Gus, who we had worked with at Smallhythe and Greenwich.

There is always something fascinating about thinking about the river in prehistory compared with the controlled and channelled version surrounded by the city that we see today. In addition our work would be relevant to the future management of the Thames. Rivers have their own cycles and fluctuations and, historically, the wider the range of information about their levels and movement the more possible it is to predict what will happen in the future. At the moment a new Thames barrier is due to be created and its height is a matter of some debate. Get that wrong, and 10 metres (33 feet) of water could cover a large

Tony and Gus sort out what's going on, while Victor begins his reconstruction.

Above: Gustav Milne on the right of picture was our key archaeologist and, importantly, was able to tell us how long we would have to dig between tides.

Opposite: Phil trying out his waders and estimating the height of a post hiding beneath the water. The archaeology begins.

part of one of the world's financial capitals. A set of Bronze Age data would add to the picture that experts on the Thames are trying to build up.

There was also a somewhat perverse attraction to excavating one or two trenches for a maximum of two hours a day. All the diggers wore wetsuits on Day One and had been briefed about the dangers of Weil's disease. We had tide watches, and safety boats were at the ready because once the tide turns it waits for no man, woman or digger – and the nearest exit point was a five-minute walk away from the site.

By 8.30 we'd targeted one particular timber with its top in relatively good condition and decided to site Trench One there. The diggers started to clear away the river gravels and mud that surrounded it. They removed this in layers so that replacing it would follow the ecologically sound plan that had been approved by the river authority. Even relatively small holes and disturbances in the river bank could have created eddies which would gradually widen and

further erode what we believed was potentially a Bronze Age land surface. In places, the modern land surface of the Thames can open up to reveal layers of brushwood and timber remains, and about 4–5 centimetres of clay and soil. At various points along the Thames this surface, which may date back to the Bronze Age or earlier, is exposed. This is a vulnerable archaeological deposit that can give us detailed information about the types of plant and fauna that were around in the prehistoric period. This material is sensitive to the water conditions – freshwater or saltwater – and so can inform us about the state of the river.

Fieldwalkers and metal detectors were used to collect any surface material on the site. They found a large number of prehistoric flints, but we were hoping that other Bronze Age objects, like the original spearhead that had been found previously, might appear.

We'd also set up a coring operation to see if the relative depth of clays and land surface could be measured. On a river like the Thames, layers of silts,

Opposite: Mr Harding in relaxation mode, booted and suited and, like a coiled spring, ready for action.

Below: All the diggers had to wear thick gloves as we'd been warned about Weil's disease. This made handling objects difficult. Here, Richard Gibb, our cameraman, is sinking quietly in the mud.

Phil examining the large number of finds from the walk on the shore. John Adams, from the Museum of London, helped to organise the fieldwalk and provided valuable background on the finds.

gravel and clay are laid down depending on the activity of the river and its interaction with the river bank. A core is taken by inserting a tube a few centimetres in diameter into the ground and withdrawing the material contained within it. This allows an archaeologist to see the different layers in section. This would eventually give us a three-dimensional picture of the landscape, showing us whether our posts were in the middle of river gravels or in an area closer to the banks, and so tell us where dry land had started in the Bronze Age. We had on hand Jane Siddell, an environmental specialist from the Museum of London Archaeological Service, who would oversee the coring and sampling of material from the excavations. We aimed to dig around two of the timbers and hopefully extract one of them.

The big question that would dominate the three days was: were we dealing with posts or piles? Posts would imply that a structure had been built on dry land with the aid of a pre-dug post hole; piles that a structure had been built out over the water and that something had been used to drive their points into the river mud. In Trench One we appeared to have a post hole – a ring of filled material around the timber – which suggested we were dealing with a post rather than a pile.

The tide turned at 10.30 on Day One and the speed with which the water rushed in surprised everyone. Kate Edwards recorded the excavation as it did so. Within an hour 6 metres (20 feet) of water would cover the site so it had to be stabilised with bags of gravel. Every time the river bank is dug, it creates new turbulence as the tide goes in and out. This can increase the erosion of a site such as ours, and so after excavating we needed to fill the holes with gravel to prevent this. Based on our observation of the tides over the previous couple of days we predicted that at least 1–2 metres (3–6½ feet) might remain when the water receded. The thought of completing our task in just another four to five hours was a daunting one!

Walking the foreshore produced large numbers of prehistoric flints, including this rather nice blade.

Removing a piece of timber to check for date rings. Unfortunately, the interior was too soft to make the sample useful.

The diggers looked exhausted and were concerned that *Time Team* might have taken on too big a task.

River mud is glutinous and would form a vacuum around the timbers because a kind of suction exists between the mud and objects in it. This would make it difficult to remove the timbers, especially as the lower down you get the more tightly packed the surrounding mud, and so the greater the suction. An added problem was that the timbers were likely to be fragile. However, it was the lower parts of the timbers that we particularly needed to see as they were likely to provide evidence – such as axe marks – that would help to date the site. The size of the axes used in the Bronze Age altered through the period, and the width of the axe cuts could be very useful.

However, we were encouraged by a couple of developments. One was seeing faint tool marks on the timber – our first sight of our Bronze Age ancestors' work – and the other was that the coring was producing excellent

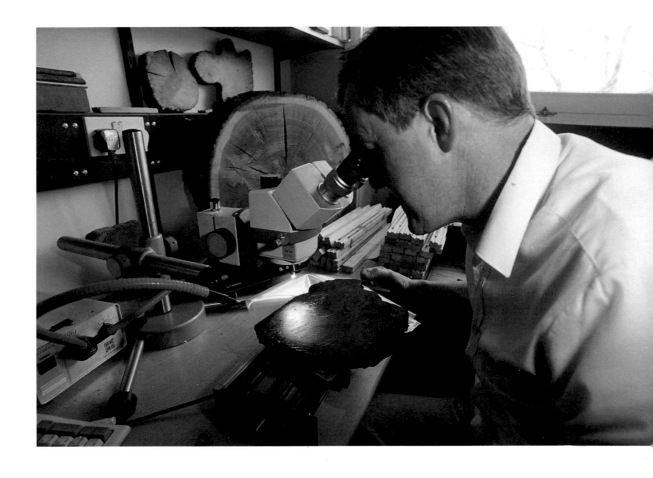

results. The cores were showing that there may have been a small emhayment

Examining the section
of timber to see if we
could help to date the post.

– a recess like a small bay – around our site and by measuring the change of
level this gave us a good idea of the likely bank shape in the prehistoric period.

The high tide gave Stewart Ainsworth and Mick a chance to explore the
Thames in a renovated Second World War Duck, which drove down the
slipway, engaged its propellers and, with a bit of a lurch, headed off towards
the Houses of Parliament. Stewart wanted to know if other islands like Thorney
Island, where Westminster Abbey stands today, had been created in the river
close to our site at Vauxhall. We were adjacent to where two ancient rivers –
the Effra and the Tybourne – had once joined the Thames, and the turbulence
caused when they joined it would have led to the Thames dropping its
sediment and creating an island. We wondered if this could have influenced
the people who had built on our site. A small island would have provided a
useful bridging point, either crossing the river or as access to a ritual platform.

Damian Goodburn was our key expert on prehistoric woodwork. He spotted a chip of oak, probably left by the Bronze Age woodworkers.

We were delighted to have Francis Pryor, an old friend of *Time Team*, whose expertise in all things Bronze Age had been essential at Flag Fen and Seahenge, on the dig. To him, the fact that the spearheads found during the first excavation had been driven deep into the mud and that their shafts were broken was evidence of a ritual deposition. However, as we pointed out, any structure which enabled people to get further out into the river, could have been useful from a number of points of view. Remembering that evidence has now been found for Bronze Age boats – the most notable being a discovery at Dover – we wondered if this could have been a quay. Bronze Age boats were capable of carrying several tons of cargo and in a tidal river a quay would allow loading and unloading over a much longer period of time.

Joining us to help with the cameo (the regular *Time Team* reconstruction), we had another familiar face: Damian Goodburn. So far as *Time Team* is concerned he is 'Mr Wood' and it was going to be his job to build the kind of pile-driver that might have driven the timbers into the mud of the river. Although no such device has ever been positively identified from the Bronze Age, the range of joints and simple blocks from the period that have been found suggests that such a device could have existed.

By 8.45 on Day Two we still weren't able to get on to the site, and Mick and Tony addressed the obvious question to Gus. He explained that heavy rain overnight had altered 'the levels in the river'. In his words, 'Predicting tidal movements is not an exact science.' As the swirling waters eddied around the site the digging team looked concerned. Had the timber survived? As the waters receded we were relieved to see that it was still there, and that the water had given the surface a good wash which enabled Damian to see the tool marks more clearly. He was also able to identify the wood chips that were coming out of the trench – which indicated that at least some of the construction work on the structure must have been done on site – as being

Working in such a small space, and with a tight margin of time, was beginning to make everybody tense. There aren't many smiles in this picture!

27

Previous page: Not something you'd see in the Thames every day.

Above: We were constantly checking the wood, both for axe marks and for signs of carving. All our effort was concentrated into this small space, and the lifting of the timber would have to take place in a very short space of time.

oak. In each black chip he could make out the medullar rays – cells which form in trees and which radiate out from the centre of an oak trunk.

We also started to find evidence of plants from the Bronze Age in the core samples. These included alder, which grows near the edge of rivers. At a site at Erith, also on the Thames, a whole Bronze Age forest is emerging from the mud. This may have been similar to that which surrounded Vauxhall. If we could identify these timbers we could begin to recreate the kind of landscape that had existed on our site.

Overnight the timber we had decided to concentrate on had developed a bit of a wobble, and the further down we went the more it wobbled. Was it loose or was there some break that wasn't visible? We managed to see that the timber was narrowing to a point – could this indicate that it was a pile? By the time the water rushed in again we had exposed more of the timber and seen a crack in it, but had not dug deep enough to extract it.

With digging stopped for the day, Mick was able to give Tony some background on diatoms. Diatoms are ingenious microscopic life forms that react differently according to whether they are in saltwater or freshwater. They are tough little characters that survive through time. Observing them through a microscope would tell us whether the water at our site had been fresh or salt during the Bronze Age. We knew we were close to what would have been the tidal head of the Thames during this period – a magical place according to Gus, where freshwater and saltwater would have met and the point to which vessels could have been swept upstream by the incoming tide and from which they would have been carried downstream as it ebbed. The presence – or absence – of diatoms would indicate whether we were below or above it.

Stewart was still working on the 'two rivers' theory and indicated that our site might be at the point where an island had been created. As we had seen from the coring evidence there appeared to have been an embayment opposite

Barney was upset that we couldn't get the whole post out, and both Mick and I did our best to look at things as positively as possible.

Above: Preparations for lifting the wood had to be carefully timed. Just poking out of the water you can see some of the other timbers.

Opposite: The new oak post marked with the Time Team logo was used to plug the hole left by the post we had removed.

the potential island. Had our structure extended over this to connect with an island or had it led out over a small peninsula created by the embayment?

As the diggers came to the end of their second excavation, Phil Harding joined Damian at the Barnes Wetland Centre, the site chosen to reconstruct a pile-driver. As Phil remarked, the centre also looked remarkably like our idea of the prehistoric Thames. His job was to trim down a trunk and remove the bark with a Bronze Age axe. This would make it easier to drag the log and would remove a potential home for fungi and infections that would cause the wood to rot more quickly. If we were able to place a post on our dig site, it would both allow us to see how such an object might be driven into river clays, and help to make good the site to avoid further erosion by refilling the hole left by the post we were going to extract (see pages 38–39).

On Day Three we had our last chance to remove the timber from the mud. However, overnight turbulence had put pressure on the crack in the upper

The critical moment came when the piece of timber was lifted.

section and the timber broke when the first small amount of force was applied. The diggers were disappointed because they had invested a lot of effort in trying to reclaim it without breaking it, but the fracture showed clearly that the crack – possibly the result of being hit by a barge or other river traffic – had cut virtually right through the timber. A last heroic effort – with only minutes remaining – saw the huge upper section lifted and at least 20 centimetres (8 inches) of the lower section exposed, but there was little hope of lifting the lower part. When the top section was lying down the Bronze Age axe marks could clearly be seen.

What did emerge in the final ten minutes of the third day's dig was that we could finally confirm that the timber was a pile. Phil was able to cut out a piece of clay and mud close to it and this showed that the section of clay surrounding the timber was too thin to have been used in a post hole. Our last act on the river bank was to refill the hole with gravel and stabilise it with the new post.

Stewart was sure that our site was at the point where the Thames, the Effra and the Tybourne had come together. Our pile would have been one of a number that supported a structure that probably bridged the embayment and made its way out to the island created by the three rivers. The size of the pile indicated to Gus that the structure had been a major one, and our own experiment with a pile-driver had underlined the amount of effort that would have been needed to drive a timber of this size into the river mud.

The evidence from the diatoms showed we were dealing with freshwater, which means the tidal head would have been above Westminster, below our site.

Our site, as Francis concluded, would have been a place of real magic for our Bronze Age ancestors. The amazing spearheads would have been placed as ritual objects at a point where the freshwater and saltwater mixed, a key position for the tidal range of the river. It is likely that this was both a crossing and a ritual site and so it could potentially be regarded as the first of London's bridges.

Above: Just prior to this, we'd discovered a major crack in its base.

Overleaf: Within two to three hours of the tide coming in, our site had once more been covered by the mighty Thames.

ELLA'S CAMEO:

A BRONZE AGE PILING RIG

Given that we were going to investigate a prehistoric wooden structure on the Thames foreshore, the most relevant cameo seemed to be to shape a similar post using early tools, and to work out how Bronze Age man would have been able to build it in situ. There are no archaeological examples from that period to work from, so I turned to Damian Goodburn, our ancient woodworking wizard, for advice.

The problem was that in order to drive a large pointed stake into the river bed or boggy shore we had to find a means of getting above the pile in order to hammer it in. Damian came up with two possibilities. Our Bronze Age ancestors could either have built a wooden platform over the site and worked from that or they could have designed a simple piling rig – which sounded like much more fun. Rigs are known to have been used by the Romans so there was no reason to believe that Bronze Age people weren't equally capable of designing something similar. The sophistication of their woodworking, as seen in their beautifully structured boats, was really impressive so there was no doubt that they had plenty of ingenuity.

All we needed for the rig were three long ash poles, carefully chosen with forks at the top end; a strong rope – we used a natural hemp but it could have been made from honeysuckle fibres or wythies; a heavy log of green oak with a lug carved into it to make the ram; and a primitive wooden pulley-block and some animal fat to grease it. For the pile itself, Damian shaved the bark off a well-grown straight oak log using a

Phil preparing the hammer for the prehistoric pile-driver.

bronze axe that was hafted as an adze. Using the tool in this way was much more efficient than using it as an axe, and created lovely scalloped flutes down the length of the timber which matched the tool marks glimpsed on the post in the Thames. That's one of the glories of these practical recreations – it is often only by working with tools that you learn how they could be used efficiently, and this can inform archaeological interpretation and understanding better than

Top: A bronze axe hafted in order to use it as an adze. This produced similar chips to the ones we had found on the site.

Bottom: The pile-driver about to be released.

all the theorising. Bronze is a soft metal that can blunt quite easily if used against the grain of wood but, worked with the grain, it can be almost as efficient as steel.

Initially we were hoping to replace the post that we were going to excavate from the Thames with our newly made one, using the piling rig on the actual site. However, the team wasn't able to remove the original post in time so we had to plant ours at the Barnes Wetland Centre in order to test out the rig. We had chosen the site because it was the most similar environment to the Bronze Age landscape with its reed beds and wonderful wildlife. It also caused a few problems because we had to be careful not to disturb the nesting birds in the sanctuary.

When we finally tested our piling rig, it was a resounding success. I had been worried because we didn't have a great height to drop the ram from – our tripod was 5 metres (16 feet) high, allowing only a 2 metre (6½ feet) drop to the top of the post – but the animal fat worked a treat on the rope and released the heavy ram very freely. You could really get a sense of the power of the machine when the ram landed on the post with a satisfying thud and, sure enough, the wood was driven into the ground inch by inch with each lift and strike of the hammer.

An aerial view showing the layout with the earlier cloister area on the right, the lawns in the distance and the north quadrangle to the left.

CHICKSANDS
BEDFORDSHIRE

'SOMETHING FAIRLY RISQUÉ WAS GOING ON IN THERE 800 YEARS AGO'

Tony Robinson's piece to camera: 'This is Chicksands in Bedfordshire. I can't tell you exactly what goes on here, except to say it's a military intelligence centre. That building over there is the officers' mess but it was once part of a thirteenth-century monastery, the site of a home-grown British order called the Gilbertines. Something fairly risqué was going on in there 800 years ago. Nuns and monks living together – it was an experiment that caused a scandal. How did it work, how were they kept apart? In recent years some walls and even the occasional burial have been found. The commanding officer has allowed us in for just three days on a mission to sort out the naughty nuns and monks of Chicksands.'

Monasticism

When the founders of Christian monasticism retreated to the Egyptian desert in the late third century, with the specific aim of distancing themselves from the bustle, noise and corruption of the outside world, they could hardly have guessed that they were to become the fathers of a movement which, a thousand years later, had become one of the wealthiest and most powerful landowners in western Europe, and counted its followers in the hundreds of thousands.

The idea of the monastic way of life spread so rapidly in western Europe that it had reached Ireland by the early fifth century and, although the evidence is sparse, it is likely that a form of monasticism reached mainland Britain by the end of the same century at the latest. In England, monastic organisation was still relatively informal up to the late Anglo-Saxon period. However, following a major root-and-branch reform of monasteries in the tenth century, most of the major communities at least had been placed on a far more formal, disciplined footing by the time of the Norman Conquest, and would have been much closer to what they were like at the height of the monastic movement in the twelfth, thirteenth and fourteenth centuries.

Today we might think that the monastic way of life could be hard and at times harsh. But it also provided security for those who made a commitment to it: although no monastery could survive in total isolation from the outside world, most of the day-to-day necessities for living, both spiritual and physical, could be supplied from within the community and from the produce of its estates. The use of rules meant that the monastic day was mapped out almost down to the last minute and it is possible that some of Europe's earliest mechanical clocks may have been used in monastic houses to help regulate the day more accurately.

The placing of the English crown on a French head after the battle of Hastings brought about numerous changes in English society, but also provided an opportunity for foreign monastic houses to gain a foothold in England. By and large these were the so-called 'reformed' orders – communities which claimed to take a far more rigid, 'back to basics' view on how the various monastic rules should be applied.

However, by no means all the new orders were imports. Some were very much home-grown. In 1147, for example, Gilbert of Sempringham in Lincolnshire founded the Gilbertines after the Cistercians had refused to take over the running of an informal house of religious women, tended by lay brothers and sisters, which he had established close to the church of which he was priest. Eventually Gilbert's order became a 'double house', sustaining both men and women, who were strictly segregated. The order failed to spread to Europe, but was extremely successful in eastern England, with 1,500 to 2,000 members when Gilbert died in 1189, and no fewer than twenty-four communities by the time of Henry VIII's dissolution of the monasteries (1536–40).

Chicksands was the third largest Gilbertine house after Sempringham itself and Watton in Yorkshire. Like the Carthusians, the particular way in which the order was run, and the separate facilities provided in the double houses for male and female members, gives rise to very distinctive archaeology with the duplication of such features as refectories and infirmaries. Indeed, at Watton, the site is effectively a 'mirror image' of itself, with two precincts each containing a church and a cloister.

It is a sobering thought that it took Henry VIII just four short years to destroy a way of life which, in Britain, had been followed in a bewildering variety of forms for over a thousand years.

I was interested in Chicksands for two main reasons: the enthusiasm of the commanding officer of the secret military base, who had initially contacted us; and being able to work on a site – a medieval monastery – that was so much in Mick Aston's and Jenni Butterworth's territory. We knew that a large part of the building occupied by the monks – or as they should more properly be known, the canons – still existed. But this was supposed to be a double house – for monks and nuns – so one part of it was missing. The nuns' quarters were likely to contain cloisters, rooms for eating and sleeping, and possibly even a hospital. But could we find it? I also felt that the likelihood of finding a cemetery would make for additional interest if the hunt for monastic cloisters proved fruitless.

Another idea that appealed to me was that Jenni should take time off from her duties as a member of our digging team and become a nun for twenty-four hours – something that took a bit of persuading. Jenni knew monasteries and knew about nuns, but she also confessed that she had a 'bit of a thing' for chaps in uniform and would therefore find it a challenge to keep her mind on higher things while she was in seclusion.

Early morning gathering on the lawns. The officer in charge of the establishment and John Ette from English Heritage check out the geophysics results.

The Gilbertines were founded by a Lincolnshire priest, Gilbert of Sempringham, in the mid-twelfth century. It promoted double houses – men and women lived in separate buildings but within the same religious community – a custom which had existed in Anglo-Saxon England. As women were thought to be the source of all evil, this was a risky enterprise and there was a little local difficulty at one of the order's monasteries, in Watton in Yorkshire – but more of that later. Male members of the Gilbertines were canons, a role that was closer to that of a priest than a monk, and were often active in local communities, in contrast to monks who were more reclusive. The canons and the nuns were served by lay brothers and sisters. Chicksands had been home to an experiment in this kind of communal living, with men and women living adjacent to each other.

Getting into the base was a complicated business and soldiers with guns and guard dogs at the ready made it clear that high security meant what it said. We all had to have passes, having given our personal details, and have our vehicles checked. However, once we were inside, the welcome and help we received from all military personnel made it worthwhile. Chicksands is a very

The exterior of the priory in all its splendour.

important historic monument, as well as being a military base, and is of guardianship standard. This means that it is of national quality and consequently English Heritage work closely with the military at Chicksands to preserve the character of the buildings and protect the archaeology, even though the site is in active use every day.

The surviving structures that make up the officers' mess would have been the main cloister used by the canons. They are beautiful thirteenth-century medieval buildings with vaulted ceilings and arches, and the main range has an incredible fifteenth-century timber roof. We needed to find the nuns' cloister, which would be bigger and grander than that of the canons.

Most plans of Gilbertine monasteries show that nuns and canons shared a church and the likely location for the nuns' cloister would therefore be to its north. This would be the most convenient location as well as being the traditional route from what was considered to be the dark side and would also

Graham Dixon and I contemplate the start of yet another Time Team shoot through his mini portable television: 'We've been together now for over ten years, and it don't seem ...'

allow the nuns to pass quickly into the church from their cloisters. At Chicksands an elaborate doorway still standing would have been the entrance to the church, and it would have made sense if the nuns' cloister had had the same sort of entrance. However, we would be using a plan based on the Gilbertine double house at Watton in Yorkshire which showed a different arrangement with a totally separate cloister.

Jenni had produced a suitably rigorous research design. A research design outlines the number and size of the trenches we are going to dig, the questions we are going to address and the goals we hope to achieve. It's important that trenches are located to answer a specific hypothesis or question. As double houses are so rare, Chicksands was an extremely important site, so we were keen to have English Heritage's support. John Ette, an inspector with English Heritage, was on hand to give his help and advice. After working with John on an earlier site at Malton in Yorkshire we were confident that we would have a good relationship with him. We were not surprised that early in Day One he was uttering the word 'surgical' a lot, as we were all anxious to be as precise as we could be with our trenches.

Barney Sloane had also joined us. His speciality is medieval burials and he had come equipped with excavation reports from 1969 which recorded that bodies had been found when a modern pipe trench was put in. It was interesting that the report referred to the fact that tiles were placed over the graves. This implied that the people who had been buried were of a high status, and also that the burials might have been inside a building, possibly in a chapel.

On Day One our search began on the lawns to the east of the main building. Aerial photographs had detected rectangular marks that could be structures and we were keen to get started. The geophysics team had also surveyed the lawns and had found an anomaly to the east – a clear target to aim at. Phil opened Trench One on the lawns in this area while Mick worked his way around the buildings to the west, avoiding large guard dogs and looking for a suitable place to dig between the canons' cloister and the northern buildings.

John Gater was soon able to locate the pipe trench and we opened Trench Two alongside the 1969 dig. With Barney's team augmented with army volunteers – 'you and you go to that trench and dig' – things were moving along nicely until Trench One came up with nothing. A bit of geology – some hardened areas in the sandstone – explained the geophysics results, but why had so few finds turned up? We decided to abandon it and to open up Trench Three on the aerial anomaly.

Overleaf: Claire Stephens with a big zimmer frame, going for depth.

Mick kept saying, 'It's to the north – it's to the north' like a monk intoning a psalm, but the problem was that a huge cobbled yard covered most of the 'north', and we couldn't risk pulling up large amounts of this without good reasons and good geophysics. Chris Gaffney was dispatched to get the ground-penetrating radar (GPR) going. Jenni had opened Trench Four between the canons' cloister and the yard but it, too, was turning up little. We were expecting walls but none were appearing.

Meanwhile, the commanding officer had taken a hand backfilling the abandoned trench on his lawn. Backfilling on Day One is not a good sign, and Tony sat down with Mick to hear why he thought all this lack of evidence was 'good news'. Mick had never really believed the plan for Watton, feeling that there were too many suppositions made to create it. It didn't back up his 'north' theory, and in his view the fact that we had found zero in Trench One was good news because it scotched the idea of an east cloister.

Opposite: The commanding officer lending a hand to backfill a trench.

Above: Mick is probably telling Victor that he thinks it's to the north, a message he was keen to tell anyone who would listen!

All this monumental lack of anything gave Robin Bush time to discuss Jenni's role as a nun, which would begin at noon the following day. He showed her a picture of a Gilbertine nun wearing a cloak that Jenni described as 'looking itchy'. The idea of Robin chatting to a potential nun was a little surreal, but he seems to have behaved himself.

Meanwhile, a small bit of wall had appeared in Trench Three, Phil's second trench on the lawn. Not wonderful – but what had also turned up was thirteenth- to fifteenth-century stained glass. Was it possible that there could be buildings to the east? Could a large monastic complex have been situated 9 metres (10 yards) from a pair of trenches that had so little in them? At the end of Day One it was north one, east a sort of quarter!

On Day Two the commanding officer confirmed his willingness to let us have a go at the cobbles. However, radar was not yet producing ideal results and Chris would have to continue the search.

Below: Careful removing of turfs was essential as the rather beautiful lawn had to be put back when we'd finished.

Opposite: Unearthing the tile-capped graves.

The secret nature of the base meant we had our own liaison officer, who proved to be invaluable when dealing with the powers that be. John Ette is studying more geophysics surveys.

Stewart Ainsworth had been trawling through maps and had turned up a reference to a field called Warren field to the east of the main building – a Sir George Osborne had owned the monastery in the nineteenth century and in 1855 he had produced a map showing various locations. And Robin had found a 1727 reference to a hospital associated with a Warren field, also to the east. Were we in the area of the hospital? It looked as though we should concentrate on the east. Another factor that was putting us off the north, archaeologically, was the apparent lack of evidence from excavations carried out there in the past.

Barney was becoming a little uncertain about whether he was dealing with graves, due to the disorganised nature of the tiled capping, but was clinging to the fact they were largely trapezoidal in shape, that is, broader at the shoulder. They also had, he said, the look of 'a rockery', but I think he may have been going through a bad patch.

At midday Jenni's digging was over for the day and she was joined by our 'nuns'. The first shock came when she found she couldn't wear any knickers under her habit. The second came when she saw a computer-generated image of herself with her head shaved. The idea behind the habit was that it defeminised the woman wearing it by disguising her body shape. Jenni would have to look down at all times during her twenty-four hours as a nun, and take a vow of silence. Her first meal was pottage – a sort of weak stew made from water, vegetables and barley – and a lump of hard bread. Professor Roberta Gilchrist from Reading University had joined us as a key expert. She used the term 'holy anorexia' and explained that nuns were always fairly close to starving in order to 'tame' and 'defeat' their bodies. During the evening and night Jenni would be woken to pray. Any deviation from the rule would be punished. Jenni explained to me how it was organised as I wasn't allowed in there. Every hour of the day and night was divided into cycles of prayer, meditation and work. Jenni was given the *Life of St Gilbert* to read, and lots of linen headscarves and napkins to hem. Although Jenni found learning and reciting the Latin prayers interesting, she found the long services painful, even on digging-hardy knees.

Local volunteer pot washers are invaluable to us. The number of finds they need to process can be amazing.

At 2.00, back in the real world, Mick and Stewart were looking at the view from the chopper and airing the 'east versus north' debate. John, meanwhile, was showing Roberta a whole set of geophysics to the east of where Phil was digging. She thought they indicated potential buildings and with John Ette's agreement we decided to pursue them by opening a further trench.

Four tile-capped burials had appeared in Barney's trench, and Roberta confirmed that such graves were not common and that tiles implied high status. Also, it was possible that the burials were next to a path so that the graves could be seen.

Trench Three, which had been opened on John's anomaly, had soon started to reveal stonework made of what John Ette called 'clunch' – a hard local form of chalk. It was looking good for a possible medieval building. By the end of the day, stonework of high quality was appearing including window sections with grooves for glazing bars.

Mick about to take off with Stewart in the helicopter – always a favourite moment for him.

With a quick thought for Jenni entering her first night as a nun, we headed for G&Ts in the officers' mess.

Katie Hirst was able to pay a quick visit to Jenni, who had begun to get into the experience. In her own words: 'I feel strange – I don't know what time it is. You have to keep your eyes down – I feel guilty looking at you … It's so structured – it's easy to be withdrawn.' Jenni still had twelve hours to go …

On Day Three we started to find very nice pieces of medieval pottery, and more stained glass. The stonework in Trench Three, John's 'anomaly' trench, had begun to look really exciting and Mick suggested widening the hole in an attempt to find floor tiles that might help to date the site.

Barney had at last reached bones but they appeared to be a jumble of broken-up remains. Osteologist Professor Margaret Cox identified a bone that had been cut when a new grave had been dug over the one in which it was found. Did we just have holes with large numbers of disarticulated skeletons?

Invited into the officers' mess, Phil was deemed to be inappropriately dressed. The commanding officer gave him this Mickey Mouse tie, so that he could be served a drink. I've not seen Phil wearing it since.

It was time to observe Jenni's progress. Later she would tell us how she began to feel: 'Being woken at 2 a.m. was OK,' she told us, 'but 4 a.m. was bad.' She had found that her mood had changed – she wasn't ready to get up again. 'I was really hungry and tired – it felt much harder to concentrate on what I was trying to do.' She had to wash without taking off her habit – nuns weren't allowed to see their own bodies... After breakfast at 7 o'clock she attended Mass. 'There was the strange disembodied voice of a canon coming from the other side of a wall – we were cut off from men, but we still needed a man to say Mass.'

At the start of Day Three, Tony had caught up with Robin to hear about an event that had shaken the monastic world in the twelfth century. The story of the nun of Watton was so extreme that Mick – not normally noted for shyness – had been reluctant to tell me about it. The main thread, as told by Robin, was as follows:

Opposite: Jenni trying to look innocent enough to be a nun, and just about managing it!

Above: We were beginning to move serious amounts of spoil, and in some cases, there appeared to be very little in it.

'A young girl was committed to a nunnery at the age of four and grew up in the community. She had not gone there of her own free will and had little sense of vocation. As a young woman she was seduced by one of the canons and became pregnant. The culprit was caught and physically punished by the nuns, in a way that would make your eyes water. The pregnant nun was imprisoned in chains in a walled-up room. In her cell she had a vision of the archbishop of York and her chains fell away and her pregnancy disappeared. She was reinstated as a nun but her story shocked the medieval world and influenced the severity of Gilbertine rule.'

For Jenni, life had become harder on the final morning. When she dropped her book while reading the scriptures she had to confess her action and was made to lie prostrate on the floor. As she said later: 'I thought I could just rest in this postion but it was very uncomfortable.' At noon she was free. 'I need a bag of crisps,' were her final words to her fellow nuns, and she made

Dennis Borrow, one of Time Team's long-serving camera men, catches Tony looking pleased about one of our first artefacts.

TRENCH TEN REPORT

On the afternoon of Day Three, geophysics picked up a 'noisy' anomaly suggesting a large structure below the turf. An enormous pier foundation with beautiful pillar bases and a floor surface of compacted chalk was exposed, indicating that we had probably located the edge of the cloister within an infirmary complex. The workmanship of the stonework and the size of the structure surprised us all, and indicated that the infirmary was a high-status and well-founded building that served the priory community. The huge structure would have supported a vaulted ceiling around the cloister walkway, which we knew could have been accessed through a spiral staircase the very bottom of which was found to the north in Trench Eleven. It rapidly became the most evocative structure found on the site.

The stratigraphically earliest event in Trench Ten was the construction of the pier base foundation (1009). The structure was formed from a rubble core bonded with hard, lime-based mortar with very well-dressed ashlars on the external face.

A compacted chalk and limestone floor surface (1007) immediately below a layer of fine sand (1004) lay around the base of the foundations. Together these represent the surviving floor surfaces within the cloister walk.

Immediately above (1004), was a 0.7-metre (27½-inch) thick deposit of demolition rubble (1003), a mixture of stone, mortar, carved window frames and tile, which had fallen around the foundations as the infirmary was demolished.

A later addition to the building was wall (1008), aligned north–south and also constructed over the earlier floor surface (1004). The construction of the wall was very different to the surrounding masonry, with pebbles and reused tile forming the core, with undressed ashlars on its face. The time span between these two events is unclear, largely because the dig was so close to its time deadline.

To the east of the cloister wall was a 0.7-metre (27½-inch) deep deposit of demolition rubble (1001), containing large limestone cobbles, worked stone and chunks of mortar. Below this was another demolition layer (1002), a greyish-brown, loose silt containing fragments of mortar and occasional pieces of stone.

The interpretation of this building is affected to a large extent by a shortage of time and the small percentage of foundations exposed. Although it is likely that these remains are those of a cloistered infirmary building, exposing the remainder of the structure and seeing the entire foundations in plan would be necessary to confirm this view.

a quiet and chastened passage to the dinner-bus for a large piece of fish with loads of potatoes. Later, she talked about how she had begun to withdraw and didn't want to talk to anyone from the outside world – Katie's visit was almost an intrusion.

We had now started to find medieval tiles and pieces of an important building under the lawns. Our medieval-buildings expert, Richard Morriss, identified them as being from the twelfth to thirteenth centuries, possibly from a cloister but they were probably not big enough to be from the main building. He noted the 'crispness' of the stonework.

Barney finally found a complete skeleton 1.2 metres (4 feet) down. Margaret said it was that of an older male. This meant that, with the bones that had already been found, the site was unlikely to be that of a monastic segregated cemetery because men, women and children had been found. However, the tiles on the graves indicated that it had been a high-status

Opposite: One of Barney's skeletons.

Above: The fragility of the skeletons meant that they had to be excavated from board stretched across the trenches.

A splendid piece of medieval architecture.

burial place. One of the graves could have been that of a wealthy benefactor of the monastery.

Day Three saw a final push to confirm that our building remains were part of the nuns' cloister. Mick was still keen on the hospital theory because he couldn't accept that the cloister would be anywhere but to the north and Stewart agreed. What we had discovered, however, was some of the best-preserved medieval architecture ever found in Britain, and Phil had a final surprise. A set of flat stones in Trench One, slightly triangular in shape, had puzzled him but Mick, from a perspective outside and above the trench, recognised it as what remained of a staircase that had spiralled around a central column.

Even on Day Three we were still trying to pursue the north option. The GPR located structures below the cobbled yard to the north, but these were at a level well below those discovered by previous excavations. Mick and Stewart both

thought the cloister should be in that direction, but a small trench slipped in adjacent to the cobbled yard held nothing. The material we had found in Phil's trench was clearly part of a high-status monastic building. Two or three pieces here suggested to Richard Morriss that a cloister could possibly have been built in this area. However, Mick still felt that there was insufficient evidence to convincingly say that this was where the nuns' main building was located. Nevertheless the officers of the base would have to start viewing their lawns in an entirely new light.

From my point of view, I was delighted that we'd found something spectacular for the commanding officer and the base, and in many ways the experience of watching Jenni act out her role as a nun so close to the site of her medieval predecessors was fascinating. She confessed that her main thought was that she would speak less in the future, but I'm happy to say that's one vow that was broken fairly quickly.

Phil explaining to Mick how far he has to go down before he hits the archaeology.

65

Ella's Cameo:
A day in the life of a Gilbertine nun

Movements had to be carefully directed in order to fit in with the drawings which Jenni could not see.

This was one of the trickiest cameos I've ever had to produce. The aim was to try to give Jenni as full an experience as possible of life in a thirteenth-century abbey. As we didn't have access to an abbey or real nuns Graham Dixon, the director, decided to work against a plain blue screen, using a huge deserted gym in the army camp as our studio and re-enactors from the White Company as the extra nuns. Victor would draw in the backgrounds in post-production – very effective in the final film, but giving Jenni little sense of reality when she was on the set.

We had Victor's rough sketches to work with, but there was a lot of fiddling to get the perspectives to work when real people were involved. The main problem was that each scene entailed meticulous framing and lighting in order to work visually and therefore had to be heavily directed from the technical angle. This was completely at odds with the cloistered, silent, religious life of repetitive prayer and uninterrupted contemplation that I was trying to provide for Jenni. Even simple actions created real dilemmas. Formally washing her hands in the lavatorium before prayer is an example. Victor had drawn a water spout and stone trough on the wall in his background, so I had to decide whether to ask Jenni to pretend to wash her hands in exactly the right place in mid-air so that it looked effective in post-production, or give her a basin of water so that it would feel much more real for her at the time. In the end, both versions were used.

We tried to set up the shots with the White Company nuns first, so that Jenni was disturbed as little as possible. Nobody was allowed to speak to her apart from myself when I absolutely had to, and other nuns if it was appropriate. My main objective was to allow her to experience the gruelling twenty-four-hour routine as authentically as possible. This entailed praying in church eight times during the day and night (which meant that I also managed to get only three hours sleep at a time); eating only small amounts of simple, tasteless gruel and drinking watered-down beer; wearing the uncomfortable habit and headdress of a nun day and night; and sleeping on a straw mattress – complete, as it turned out, with fleas! Learning Latin prayers and reading extracts from the *Life of St Gilbert* were probably the highlights of her day, and the use of a toothbrush and a modern lavatory were the only concessions she was allowed.

It had been surprisingly difficult to glean the information about how a Gilbertine nun actually filled her day. Historians hadn't addressed the subject in any detail and the Gilbertine constitution, printed in the *Monasticon Anglicanum*, had long lists of things the nuns couldn't do, but very little about what they actually did. Finding answers to such questions as whether services were chanted or spoken, or when a nun was allowed to remove her wimple, proved to be a real challenge. I worked from the modern Benedictine orders and known structures of prayer for medieval Benedictine monks. I also took lots of advice from Professsor Roberta Gilchrist, who is head of the archaeology department at Reading University and has written many books on monasticism and religious women in the Middle Ages, and from Juliet Griffin, a re-enactor from the White Company who had researched the subject before and was providing the nuns, habits and medieval props and food for the occasion. However, some of the cameo had to be informed guesswork.

The most rewarding moment for me was hearing Jenni's reaction to the whole experience when it was all over. She had gained so much more from her ordeal than I could have hoped for, and was full of thought-provoking insights and unexpected details about her feelings during the twenty-four hours – for instance, because she wasn't allowed to make eye contact, she had felt really introverted and hemmed in. There would have been no other way for her to gain such an understanding of a nun's life and it completely vindicated all the worry, hard work and sleepless-ness that had gone into creating the cameo.

The blue-screen studio, erected to provide a background on which computer images could be added.

The cellar underneath the pub – the wall on the left was later to be knocked down.

LEIGHTON
SHROPSHIRE

'300 YEARS AGO THIS PLACE WOULD HAVE BEEN FULL OF NOISE AND ACTIVITY'

Tony Robinson's piece to camera: 'It's 8.30 in the morning and I'm in the middle of Shropshire looking for a pub! This is the Kynnersley Arms in Leighton, a couple of miles down the road is Ironbridge where most people believe the Industrial Revolution began. And this is it – it may not look like much now, but 300 years ago this place would have been full of noise and activity and the most incredible heat, because this was a blast furnace, used for making iron. We know the kind of things they would have made – things like these cannonballs [holds up cannonball] – but how exactly did they make them? Because something may have been happening here that changed the course of industrial history for ever.'

Ironbridge

If there were a league table for industrial wonders of the world, the famous iron bridge at Coalbrookdale in Shropshire would have to come very close to the top. Because the bridge was at the cutting edge of late eighteenth-century technology in its use of cast iron, the men who built it did so using the only construction methods they knew: those of the carpenter. It is in effect a wooden bridge made of iron. But the lessons were quickly learned and once the early pioneers had come to terms with the amazing structural qualities of the new material, it spawned its own particular methods of construction and caught on rapidly. The second iron bridge was erected over the Severn by Thomas Telford in 1796, at Buildwas, just two miles upstream from Ironbridge; and in 1798, an elegant bridge cast from Coalbrookdale iron was built across the River Parrett at Bridgwater in Somerset.

So many new industrial processes and manufacturing techniques were pioneered in Coalbrookdale and the Ironbridge Gorge that it really is no exaggeration to call this part of Britain the cradle of the Industrial Revolution. The industrial works cover a vast area, and after intense archaeological research over the past thirty years much of this has been incorporated in the Ironbridge Gorge Museum. The industrial remains here are so internationally important that a two-mile stretch of the Ironbridge Gorge, including Coalbrookdale, has been awarded World Heritage Site status by UNESCO.

Abraham Darby I pioneered the use of coke, rather than charcoal, to smelt iron in 1709. But the impact of Darby's development was not immediate. Initially, the quality of his iron was not as good as that smelted with charcoal in the traditional way, and he could only produce a limited quantity. Nor was there any real commercial necessity for coke-smelted iron – recent research has shown that, contrary to what was once believed, there was no shortage of wood for charcoal-making at the beginning of the eighteenth century. In fact, even in the middle of the century only four iron-making blast furnaces used the new coke-smelting process – and two of these were outside Coalbrookdale. None the less, when both the quality problems and the prejudice of other ironmasters – who were reluctant to accept that coke-smelted iron could ever be as good as pig iron made with charcoal – had been overcome, the output of iron made with coke increased massively. The iron-making industry began to gravitate away from the old charcoal areas, such as the Forest of Dean and the Weald, to establish itself firmly in the coalfields.

Darby's various innovations and Coalbrookdale's importance as an iron-making centre should be seen against the background of a long tradition of iron-making in this part of the upper Severn valley – one that goes back to at least the 1530s, when a so-called 'bloomery' was in operation at Coalbrookdale. This was a type of furnace that produced 'blooms' of iron – shapeless lumps of very impure metal, contaminated with slag which had to be removed by hammering. It is rather ironic that this early example of iron-making was located in Coalbrookdale for the same reason that there were furnaces in the Weald and the Forest of Dean: a plentiful supply of wood. Before Darby, woodland and iron ran hand in hand. It was charcoal that gave birth to Coalbrookdale's iron industry, just as it was a Coalbrookdale innovation that ultimately severed those ties.

Above: Tony and Mick contemplating the joys of archaeology.

Opposite: The crew stand in astonishment as they realise that we've got a location in the grounds of a pub.

ime Team had initially been contacted by the landlady of the Kynnersley Arms, who was fascinated by the archaeology that her pub had been built on top of, and we had also spoken to local archaeologists. The pub location had an instant appeal – Ben Frow, the commissioning editor at Channel 4, had immediately picked up on that. Also, industrial archaeology is a fascinating subject and, as it is not part of mainstream archaeology, the site would give us a slightly different set of circumstances to many of our other digs.

I was also keen to have a site where Stewart Ainsworth and Henry Chapman could have a go at what they do best: setting the central archaeological goal within its landscape context. The furnace and pub had been at the centre of a process that began with the utilisation of the landscape and natural resources and ended with objects like cannonballs. Could Stewart and Henry explain why the furnace had been sited where it was?

Day One saw us 'geofizzing' the car park and taking a close look at the remaining workings in the cellar. A huge nineteenth-century wheel stood in a wheel pit that might date back to the seventeenth century. Amongst the inevitable debris that accumulates in a pub cellar, including discarded furniture, we could just see the remains of the blast furnace arch. Before we could really start to investigate, we would have to clear the area out in order to see the archaeology better.

Jane Wood, the pub landlady, looked on as we began to contemplate just how much of her car park would have to go. Trenches One and Two would go in there so that we could assess whether the foundations of the back wall of the pub were sitting on the furnace structure. This could be about 5 metres (16½ feet) square and extend out into the car park. The process of making iron products involved three main areas of activity: a bellows area that pumped air into the furnace through the blowing arch; the furnace itself; and the casting beds where the molten iron was turned into 'pigs' that would be turned into finished products. The iron-ore flux and charcoal were loaded from the charging area above the furnace.

Some long-serving members of the Time Team crew: Richard Gibb, Steve Bowden and Jack Holmes, ready for action on the first day.

Historical documents had revealed that products created with Leighton iron included cannonballs as well as the usual pots and pans. In the 1640s the Civil War had created a need for shot and we had found a letter of 1642 ordering a ton of cannon, shot and 'grenados' from Leighton, which would be ferried up the River Severn to Worcester and then transported to the Royalist troops in Oxford. There was a nice reference to a Monsieur de la Roche who had been asked to create a nasty mixture of gunpowder and oils to enhance the performance of the 'grenados'. It would be good if we could find evidence of these.

What Jane had in her cellar were the remains of the blowing arch, the wheel pit and the area where the air entered the furnace, usually via a tuyère – a ceramic tube designed to funnel it into its heart. To get a better look at these we would have to remove a modern wall that had been built to fill a brickwork arch. Because the building was listed, we had had to get permission from the relevant authorities some time before the dig – something that had created a bit of a palaver and taken weeks of negotiation. We had talked to the county conservation officer, the county building archaeologist, the English

Below: The later water wheel on the right still contained water in its pit, which had to be removed.

Overleaf: The famous Ironbridge, downstream from our dig at the Kynnersley Arms.

Heritage archaeology officer and the English Heritage structural engineer, and commissioned our own structural engineer. It's good to see that it takes a lot of expert advice and legal licences to do this kind of work, but it's impossible not to feel that it can be alarmingly easy for people who, unlike us, are not prepared to play by the book and end up damaging ancient buildings.

Anyway on Day One, with everyone happy, Tony got the chance to strike the first blow at the modern wall – a voice suggested he should 'look butch' and away he went. Our cameraman Richard Gibb set up a nice shot from inside the cellar and it resulted in a great sequence as the bricks tumbled and light burst in, revealing how complex and detailed the brickwork structures were. You could get a sense of the huge water wheel turning, driving a massive pair of bellows that would have forced air into the furnace.

Running a blast furnace would have been a major operation for a village like Leighton. Once started it had to be kept going because of the high temperatures involved. Stopping and starting the process would result in vast variations in temperature which could destroy the structure of the furnace. It was also a dangerous business as there were often explosions when water

Below: Phil gets the chance to look at the blowing arch with local archaeologist Paul Belford.

Opposite: Katie Hirst getting to grips with the rubble, tons of which had to be removed before we could begin digging.

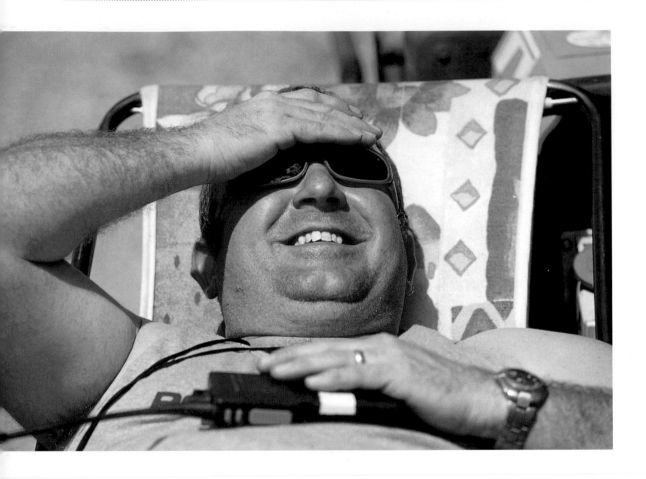

Gary our 'spark', tries to cope with the strain of the job.

leaked into the structure from the mill that drove the water wheel. Each run of five to nine months was called a 'campaign' and during the winter lay-off the interior shell of the furnace was scraped out and rebuilt.

One of the key ingredients in smelting iron was charcoal, which reaches a higher temperature than wood and has fewer impurities. Three hundred years ago the woodland around Leighton stretched for miles and vast areas were plundered for the furnace – but first the wood had to be processed. Making charcoal as it was made in the seventeenth century was to be our cameo as book I had read about making it in the Forest of Dean had implied that it could be done in three days! This was the challenge that faced Phil Harding and our two charcoal experts, who were involved with the cameo (see pages 96–97). The first step in the process is to build a clamp – a triangular structure of logs, surrounded with upright logs and finally covered with soil. The wood that is used to make the charcoal must be cooked – steamed, really – and not burned.

If too much air gets in the end result is a load of ash so the process has to be controlled. Tiny cracks in the soil have to be sealed if they threaten to let air in. Charcoal-burners do a lot of sitting and waiting and watching.

Back in the car park, Trench One was going in at a suitably safe distance from the pub wall and Phil was striking up a good relationship with Grant, the driver of the mechanical digger, and his dog Caspar. Peeling back tarmac that has been laid over what might be fragile brickwork requires skill and a watchful eye from the archaeologist. Grant proved to be a master of his trade as he took layer after layer of tarmac from the car park surface, like peeling an onion. We hit brickwork fairly soon but it looked insubstantial. I wondered if the pub had had a few dodgy outbuildings and Phil climbed into the trench to see what was going on.

John Gater's ground-penetrating radar had picked up some 'blobs' – a term that is technically different from a 'blip' and one that is to be treated with

The dog Caspar keeps an eye on his owner, Grant, while he delicately removes some of the rubble. They were a great combination.

less respect than an 'anomaly' which has a more scientific ring. Any of these can turn into a 'linear', which has the advantage of having a sense of direction but is vague in identity. Here ends this short introduction to the vagaries of geophysics vernacular. I've always thought the best guide is judging how furtive John looks when he rushes off to process the data, but all in all it's an ongoing mystery. John's 'blob' coincided with buildings Stewart and Henry had located on a post-medieval map of Leighton so we decided to put Trench Two in on this.

I had been keen to get Tony out and about with Stewart and had sent them off into head-high nettles, impenetrable undergrowth and swamps to find evidence of water management. As Henry said ruefully this was not 'prime survey country'. Water was critical to drive the wheel that drove the bellows that blew the air into the furnace, and that could also drive all manner of tools including massive hammers to forge the iron itself. Stewart and Tony were looking for evidence of dams and leats – trenches or ditches that conveyed water to mills – that would have controlled the water so that there was a regular supply to turn the wheel of the mill.

Opposite: We were gradually opening more and more of the car park. The area to the right is where the wrought iron would have run into the moulds.

Below: Phil and Victor take a wander in the woods – like an advert from a Saga catalogue.

Above: Tony and I
trying to get the details
exactly right. Gerry
McDonnell stands by to
supply necessary facts.

Opposite: Joe Ellison –
a crucial member of the
team – fully equipped to
communicate with
the world.

In the cellar, Katie Hirst, one of our diggers, had begun to excavate the mouth of the blowing area and had been joined by Rob Kinchin-Smith, an expert on industrial archaeology. They could make out the lining and were looking for the remains of the tuyère. Rob had been with *Time Team* on our heroic dig at Blaenavon in south Wales in 2000 – none of us has forgotten the sheer scale of this massive excavation – and his enthusiasm for his subject is infectious.

We knew there had been more than one mill in the area. The Domesday Book recorded a mill in Leighton and our historian, Colin Thorn, had a lease from 1630 that granted a Richard Newport the right to convert a corn mill into one for producing metal. But was it ours? It was certainly clear that long before our furnace began work there had been a number of mills grinding corn using the water-management system. The new industrialists had just adapted the earlier system and used part of its technology – the water wheel – to provide power.

I couldn't help reflecting on the transition from a wheel quietly grinding corn to an inferno of bellows, hot metal and glowing furnace. It seemed that this was the kind of place where we started manufacturing on a non-human scale. Each of the bellows could pump out 1,000 to 2,000 litres of air per blow – the equivalent of 500 people blowing simultaneously. One can only begin to imagine what life must have been like for the men who had to work in this hell-like environment.

We had by now opened up a final trench – Trench Three – in the car park and Jenni had begun to find charcoal in Trench Two. There is always one hole that needs dogged persistence and Dr Butterworth was in just the mood to provide it! As long as I kept threatening to close her trench down she would defend it to the hilt and come up with something. Phil had found archaeology in Trench One – a possible floor 2–3 metres (6½–10 feet) down – but not a lot else. There was no furnace and at the end of Day One we sat staring at a rather unlovely bit of wall that probably dated from the nineteenth century. As Phil told Tony, we just had to go deeper.

The charcoal-burners stayed at their post overnight, watching and waiting. Phil did the gentlemanly thing and brought them supplies of liquid refreshment from the pub. He also sportingly helped them to drain the refreshment so that their concentration on the steaming heap of charcoal wouldn't be interfered with unduly. I could see Phil was thinking that charcoal-burning had its compensations.

On Day Two the hunt was on for the furnace. Grant and Phil began to enlarge Trench One and prepared to remove the wall as it was sitting on top of what might be seventeenth-century archaeology. This would be a tricky business. Although we wanted to find the furnace, the wall was still archaeology and, unlovely as it was, it would have to be photographed, drawn and surveyed before being consigned to the spoil heap.

Tony paid a visit to Ironbridge to see what a complete furnace looked like, and was encouraged by the similarity between it and the remains in the pub cellar. Mick and I went to the Blist's Hill Foundry nearby. We wanted to see how objects were cast, and Mick had volunteered to try to cast a cannonball with the help of the foundry's experts in a way that would replicate what might have happened at Leighton. The details of the wooden patterns and the casting sand were fascinating. The sand is very fine and when packed around the shape that had to be cast creates a solid mould into which the iron will be poured. Watching the process, it was clear that once a furnace was roaring you would

Opposite: Deeper down in the car park, we were beginning to find the brickwork from the early furnace. Patrick McGrady and I check out the shot.

Phil was finding good evidence from the edges of the structure.

want to cast as many pieces as possible. The big difference was that at Blist's Hill we were using coke which reaches a higher temperature than charcoal.

Back at the pub, pumps were removing water from the wheel pit so that we could try to locate the tail race of the mill, and Rob had found the channel for a seventeenth-century wheel which appeared to have been about 60 centimetres (2 feet) wide. The existing nineteenth-century wheel had been enlarged to a width of about 1.2 metres (4 feet). Phil had reached a deep level in Trench One and found substantial stonework with the edge of what we thought might be an arch. Could this be the place where the molten metal had come out of the furnace?

At the foundry at Blist's Hill, Tony was on hand to see Mick's cannonball emerging from its sand cast. It was a fine job: a 24-pounder complete with 'git', the bit of metal left when the molten metal is poured into the mould – I like to think this is the origin of the expression a 'useless git'! As Tony

contemplated the finished object he commented that such an object, fired from a cannon, might give you a 'bit of a headache'.

At the charcoal clamp the pressure was on. We needed charcoal but in order to get it for Day Three it had to be extinguished now. Had there been enough time to produce any charcoal? The experts were split in their opinions, but we made the decision to pour water on the clamp and let it cool down.

A pit of charcoal had begun to appear in Trench Two. Was this the supply that had fuelled the furnace? Jenni's persistence was paying off. In Trench One we had at last found the fragile brickwork of the furnace. We would have to open up the area on the final day to see if we could find more of the structure. Stewart and Henry who had been 'geofizzing' the area since Day One were still finding remains of dams and mills from a variety of periods close to the site, and had promised something special for Day Three. Rob had reached the bottom of the wheel pit and was looking for finds in the sludge.

Above: Trying to find the outlet for the water. Robert Kinchin-Smith pokes around in the murk.

Overleaf: The trench in the car park, looking down directly on the site where the blast furnace once burned.

Day Three saw more of the casting area being exposed in Trench One and Phil could see a large void behind some rubble that might be the mouth to the casting beds. He became increasingly excited as he realised that he was indeed getting closer to it. We would be limited by the foundations of the pub walls, but he was able to see a curve in the well-made stonework and, eventually, a channel that would have led the molten metal away.

Gerry McDonnell, our metals expert, had been testing the metalwork and slag from the area of the excavation and had found no evidence that coke had been used at Leighton. Slag provides invaluable evidence of the effects of the iron-making process. The better the quality of the furnace, the more impurities there are extracted in the slag. This meant that our furnace was one of the last charcoal ones to be in use before the change to coke. As Tony's voice-over says: 'Whilst the pioneers down the road at Ironbridge were forging the future, our furnace was stuck in the past. Phil's digging up a dinosaur.'

The search for a wider geographical context was still producing results. In the woods Stewart had found a trackway and a beautiful bridge, referred to in

Below: Final day and we try to summarise the results.

Opposite: The mouth of the furnace can just be seen to the right. From here, the molten metal would have streamed out.

a seventeenth-century document, that had been created to allow Royalists to transport cannon shot from Leighton to the Severn.

The clamp was finally opened and, although it looked as though the early damping down had affected the amount of charcoal it produced, we did have enough for the final team barbecue.

The finds on Day Three included a pipe stem dated c.1660 and made by George Hartshorn, which had possibly belonged to one of the workers and had been used by him while he waited for the iron to cool.

Ian Powlesland and Katie had excavated around the stonework in the cellar. This had now been cleared of debris and we could see what a superb structure the furnace was. Outside in the car park Phil could stand in a substantial portion of the furnace, which we hope will be preserved. The Kynnersley Arms now has another attraction apart from its excellent beer – its own unique monument to the early days of the Industrial Revolution.

Opposite: Phil was keen to find as much as the furnace as possible on the final day.

Below: Working out the vital final piece to camera.

ELLA'S CAMEO:
CHARCOAL-BURNING

I've always taken charcoal for granted, as a necessary component in all the metalworking experiments *Time Team* has done over the years, but before I researched this project I'd never stopped to consider how it was made. The facts are fascinating. Wood burns at about 300° Centigrade (570° Fahrenheit), and by transforming it into almost pure carbon through a process of controlled cooking in an earthen clamp it is possible to end up with a fuel capable of burning at 1200°– 400° Centigrade (2190°–2550° Fahrenheit). It seems like magic – if it works.

Phil hacking into the clamp, a shot that nicely captures the drama of the moment.

From the outset we had major problems with the time scale, trying to push a process that normally takes between five and seven days into the three-day filming schedule. It was difficult to find anyone who was prepared to take on such a challenge but we ended up with a great team. Paul Pinnington is a modern charcoal-burner and is used to working with a kind of huge metal dustbin that he simply packs with wood, closes up and leaves to 'cook' safely for several days without having to tend it through the night. He'd never attempted to use the old-fashioned method, so he brought in Jonathan Roberts from the Weald and Downland Open Air Museum who had experimented with small earth clamps before. Both were willing to put their reputations on the line – and, more importantly, to stay up in the woods all night, tending the fire and patching the earthen walls as they cracked. (A stray gust of wind could cause the fire to break

out at any time if there were cracks and everything would go up in flames.)

It felt like a true experiment with lots of potential for failure, which always makes a cameo more interesting. There were so many variables that could affect the outcome: the type of trees the wood came from; the thickness of the wood; the size of the clamp; the dampness of the wood; and the wind and weather conditions. The main difficulty was that once the clamp had been built and lit, we couldn't look inside it to see how the process was going. We had to rely on Jonathan's experience in judging the colour and quality of the steam and smoke being driven off by the heat. I felt sorry for him because he sensed that we hadn't achieved the right colour smoke before the top of the clamp was closed in – but had to make the decision to close it in order to have a chance of

finishing the 'cooking' in time for us to open the clamp and see the results before the end of filming. There was also the possibility that, as a result of stoking the fire for too long before covering it, too much of the wood might have been burnt in the initial stages and there would be nothing left to convert to charcoal. The dilemmas felt very real.

We knew that the wood we were using was not really dry enough, and it was exciting not knowing whether or not we had succeeded until we finally opened the clamp. We made bets on the percentage of charcoal we'd managed to make, but it turned out that we had all been wildly optimistic. In conventional terms, the charcoal-burning was a bit of a disaster. The wood hadn't caught sufficiently alight initially, because the kindling was also too damp, and only the top part of the stack had been successfully turned into charcoal – but we did salvage enough to have a barbecue! It was a great experiment and I think we learnt more about the process by experiencing all the problems, and worrying about potential disasters, than we would have done if everything had gone perfectly.

Top: Clamp watching. Phil with our two experts getting ready to sort out the charcoal.

Bottom: Preparing the charcoal clamp in the forest.

The massive earthworks around the main house
at High Ercall Hall.

HIGH ERCALL

SHROPSHIRE

'355 YEARS AGO, ROYALIST TROOPS WERE FIGHTING FOR THEIR LIVES.'

Tony Robinson's piece to camera: 'This is High Ercall Hall in Shropshire – today it's the very picture of rural tranquillity but 355 years ago, at the height of the Civil War, more than 200 Royalist troops were crammed inside the walls fighting for their lives. They'd already survived two bloody sieges but the final attack was to prove too much. The strategic fortress was to fall into Parliamentary hands. Just how it finally succumbed to the Roundhead guns is a bit of a mystery, but it is not the only mystery here. There is a plaque on the wall saying the hall was built in 1608, but you have to ask, "What's this bit of medieval monastery doing here?" And then there are those massive earthworks. The Royalist troops depended on the fortification, but could they be much older than that? *Time Team* have been invited here to unravel the mystery of High Ercall Hall and, as usual, we've got just three days to do it.'

Medieval Moated Sites

Most people understandably expect every self-respecting, major stone-built castle to possess a moat and, by and large, most do – although by no means all moats were 'wet' ones filled with water. However, in addition to these great buildings there grew up a whole class of smaller, rural, defended settlements that archaeologists tend to lump together under the general term 'medieval moated sites'.

It has been known for many years that these sites exist, but it was the early 1960s before archaeologists appreciated that they form a distinct class of field monument in their own right. Since then an increasing amount of fieldwork and documentary study, and the use of aerial photography, have shown that they survive in remarkably large numbers. Well over 5,000 have already been identified in England, and new discoveries are made every year. Although only a relatively small number have been excavated, it is enough to show a clear consistency in the dating. It seems that most of the sites fall into the period from the very early thirteenth century to about the mid-fourteenth. They also show a distinct distribution. While moated sites are known in virtually every corner of England they appear to cluster in areas where clay soils provided an effective water sealant. The West Midlands, Suffolk and Essex, for example, possess especially large numbers.

The defensive aspect of their construction was probably only a minor consideration, and determined attackers would not have been deterred for long. Rather, it looks as though in many cases the building of a moat was intended for show, as a mark of status within the neighbourhood: the medieval equivalent of a Ferrari parked in the garage. It cannot be coincidence that most of the known moats seem to coincide with land that was owned by manorial lords – men who would not have been in the top rank of secular landowners, but who instead expressed their aspirations by aping their far wealthier, castle-building social superiors.

However, in some areas there may be another reason why settlements had moats. Archaeologists recently investigated a small group of sites that date from the thirteenth century and lay on what were then the flat, marshy Avon Levels, west of Bristol. These were probably individual 'colonising' farmsteads, intended to open up and exploit the potentially rich resources to be found in this wetland environment. There would have been a constant danger of inundation and one of the excavators commented that, 'the moats in this … context are probably intended primarily for drainage rather than defence or status'.

It seems as though their connotations of status were still recognised after the medieval period, and many were occupied, although not always continuously, until well into the seventeenth century, with improvements in the standard of accommodation. For example, at Bassingham in Lincolnshire a thirteenth-century moated site with an aisled hall was abandoned in the fifteenth and sixteenth centuries, but refurbished in the seventeenth. The hall was enlarged and a new floor was put down. A map from the mid-seventeenth century shows a big house surrounded by four smaller buildings. It is this later history that provided the background to *Time Team*'s investigations at High Ercall, as many surviving and upgraded moated sites were hurriedly re-fortified at the time of the Civil War. Their eventual fate would largely have depended on the loyalties of their owners during that period.

igh Ercall Hall is an impressive red sandstone building which the owner, Peter Burnett, has been renovating for three years. He believed it was built in 1608 by the Newport family, one of the largest landowners in Shropshire, and it was the site of three bloody sieges during the English Civil War in the mid-seventeenth century. Peter had an engraving of the house in the nineteenth century showing a set of turrets and colonnades, most of which have disappeared except for some arches that are now in the middle of the lawn. Had the arches been moved from their original site, and what had happened to the grandiose bits?

On Day One Mick Aston and Richard Morriss, our buildings expert, started by examining the arches in the garden. Mick wondered if they could be medieval but Richard was certain they were typical local architecture from around 1600 to 1610 as they were very similar to parts of the Market House in Shrewsbury which dates from the same period. Mick decided to place a trench at one end of the arches to see if any foundations could be located. Trench One was the first of many holes that would go into Peter's neat lawns.

Below: The usual tricky business at the beginning of a dig. Trying to interpret the geophysics results and decide where to put in our first trench. Sarah Walmsley, assistant producer, is on the left.

Opposite: The arches in the foreground appeared to be remnants of an older building. Had they been moved? Where was the rest of the building?

The fields surrounding the house are dominated by a huge earthwork, with stonework jutting out from one end, that had possibly originated as a medieval moat. Glenn Foard, an expert on Civil War archaeology had joined *Time Team* and he organised local metal detectors to search its surface for shot and other Civil War metalwork. I was concerned to get a trench into the massive bank as soon as possible to see if we could find any medieval structures and to get a possible date for the stonework in that part of the grounds. Any attack on the house would have taken advantage of the flat land opposite it and the ditch and bank therefore had to be incredibly deep. Robin Bush pointed out that the site would have been difficult to defend and that no Royalist strategist would have chosen to confront the Roundheads at High Ercall. The Parliamentarians had forced the issue by deciding to target the house simply because the Newports were a powerful and wealthy Royalist family. We hoped that Trench Two would unpick the earthwork that had withstood three sieges.

Phil Harding sorted out Trench One and found that there was only a shallow foundation of rubble for the arches, which implied they had been moved from another location. The remains of another wing of the house should have been

This year we have always made sure that spoil and trenches have been checked with a metal detector. In this case, Uncle Joe did the honours.

somewhere in the garden and we decided to place Trenches Three and Four nearer to the main building. There was a certain amount of debate between the diggers in Trench Two about the possibility of garden features. Although the Newport family had enjoyed adding gardens to their houses, this seemed to be at odds with the Civil War story we were trying to tell.

Stewart Ainsworth had discovered that there were no local buildings dating from the seventeenth century, probably because the Royalists needed to have a clear line of fire – and possibly because, as the Civil War developed, the Newports had not been afraid to take dramatic action against surrounding villages to make sure buildings weren't being used by Parliamentarian troops. Robin, who had been given a roving brief to look for dating evidence on the existing building, found some letters exchanged by Lady Diana Newport and her mother Lady Bedford which show how the war affected members of the family. One sent to Lady Newport, while she was besieged in High Ercall Hall, read: 'I know not how to give you comfort. … They did not give you good advice who told you to stay. Have a care of your little boy and come away.' The Parliamentary forces attacked High Ercall and laid siege to it for the

Medieval stonework at the base of the Civil War defences.

first time, but were beaten off by Royalist forces. As Tony put it: 1–0 to the Cavaliers!

Robin also found two wall plaques, both with dates. One in the gable referred to Francis Newport building a 'mansion' in 1608 at the age of fifty-two, but Richard wasn't convinced. He felt that the present house was not grand enough to have been described in this way. Another plaque in a nearby wall referred to building on the site in 1617. We now had a house that was apparently older than its date stamp, and a missing mansion that Richard believed the Newports should have lived in.

Jenni Butterworth had begun to find substantial pieces of wall in Trench Three, on the lawn. These could just be the first sign of the Newports' grand mansion, but were they sufficient for us to regard them as being more than demolition rubble? We all agreed that we needed to have large trenches, as otherwise we would end up with small pieces of wall that had no apparent links with each other so Trench Three would have to be made bigger.

Trench Two on the earthwork began to reveal much larger footings for the possible tower. Could they be medieval? And the metal detectors were

Opposite: Kate Edwards, as well as having to write up all the Time Team reports, is always ready to lend a hand with excavating or, as in this case, shifting a bit of lawn.

Below: Mick getting to grips with the key archaeological questions. Phil wondering when he's going to get his hands on his pint!

The cannon in position and ready to fire as part of the cameo. Cameraman Damian Eggs stands by.

beginning to find lead shot on spoil heaps around the trench, a constant reminder that we were on the site of a particularly bloody battle.

Day Two began with some encouraging signs of good-quality stonework in Jenni's trench – Trench Three – and we decided to look inside the existing house to solve the puzzle of its conflicting dates. Its top floor is known as 'the barracks' and is where at least some of the Royalist troops were stationed. We knew that at least 200 men had defended High Ercall so they must have been in every other room in the house as well. The main roof appeared to have two different designs: a larger scale cruck-built set of timbers and a smaller group of beams, one of which Richard recognised as an 'arch-braced collar truss'. It is possible to date joints like these, but we had on hand 'Mick the Dig' (Mick Worthington) in his incarnation as 'Mick the Twig' ace dendrochronologist, who was keen to drill cores out of the roof and sort out the dating.

Back in Trench Two we had our first important find: a piece of beautiful medieval floor tile. Richard referred to it as being of high status, possibly from a chapel or a hall. Kerry Ely had been working his way through the various layers in the trench and we were beginning to realise just how much earth had been piled up. In order to get a clear view of this in section we decided to cut a large trench – Trench Six –through the top layers of the earthwork. The bank had been the scene of a sad event during one of the sieges. Every day, a Parliamentarian drummer climbed up a large birch tree on the earthwork opposite and beat out a request for the king's men to retreat. Eventually, however, a Royalist called Hurlestone became so exasperated with this daily ritual that he killed the drummer with a single shot!

On the lawn two more trenches – Four and Five – had drawn a blank and we had moved closer to the main building. A 'raggle' (an area of damaged brickwork where, in the past, one wall was connected with another) on one of its walls might have been created by the earlier connecting structure – possibly part of a long gallery that provided a place for winter entertainments. Jenni had located a much bigger wall in Trench Three. However, although the

Letting fly with a matchlock – the noise seemed to be unbelievably loud. The canisters on the bandelier contain gunpowder.

stonework was high quality it was not diagnostic of a specific date – Richard described it as 'generic moulding'. This meant we couldn't say whether or not we were digging the missing grand mansion.

After hearing the story about the unfortunate drummer, Robin was intrigued to find out more about the accuracy of muzzle-loading guns, and he and Glenn went to a firing range to see how close one of these could get to a target at 50 to 100 metres (55 to 110 yards). They were also able to test the effect of shot on sandstone walls. The marksman at the range fired at a large piece of sandstone of a similar structure to that used in High Ercall Hall. The effect was spectacular: the shot splattered and left a deep pockmarked impression. It was these pockmarks that would provide a vital clue for Stewart and Glenn later in the day.

Trench Two continued to supply more details about the work that had been done to make that side of High Ercall siege-proof. It appeared that the

Opposite: Phil examining the results of a direct hit.

Below: Medieval floor tile with beautiful design.

original medieval moated manor house, which possibly had a wall and a small tower, had been reinforced with tons of sand and soil up to 4 metres (13 feet) thick in places. This increased the height of the bank and created a platform from which the Royalists could fight back against their attackers. In addition, the soil would have absorbed the power of the cannonballs fired by the Parliamentary troops.

The fortification certainly proved itself during the first siege of High Ercall Hall, and continued to do so during the second which turned into another victory for the Cavaliers. On this occasion, the Royalist Sir William Vaughan, with 900 troops and forty dragoons, attacked the Parliamentarian forces who then fled. More than 500 Roundheads were killed, captured or drowned. 2–0 to the Cavaliers.

We were also exploring the use of gabions. These are wicker baskets filled with earth and from the fifteenth to the nineteenth centuries they were used throughout Europe to strengthen fortifications. Phil was able to watch an expert basket-maker weave a beautiful basket out of wythies. He was less impressed by the gabions made by the re-enactors. These looked like pieces of

Below: Evidence of malign intent. Lead shot from the Civil War, including some flattened by walls or bodies.

Opposite: Mick and Tony looking at the start of the building remains from the Civil War. Digger Gary Burgess managed, without fail, to pick the toughest trench on every dig he came to this year.

dodgy knitting and would have to prove that they were up to the job on Day Three when a cannonball would be fired at them (see pages 124–125).

By now Stewart thought that the main Parliamentary attack on the Royalists had probably come from the south. There was no visible damage on the house, but the church was covered with pockmarks. The arches in the garden were also splattered with similar marks, and now that Stewart and Glenn knew they came from shot – thanks to Robin's investigation into muzzle-loading guns – an approach from the south became the most likely option. 'Mick the Twig' had some results from the dendro samples from the roof. The larger timbers had been felled in the spring of 1595 and the smaller ones in 1608, which meant there had been two phases of building which explained the two plaques.

On Day Three we began to find tiled floors in the trenches on the lawn, and the hunt was on for the wall that extended furthest south from the

Opposite: Mick the Twig drilling for cores to help date the interior of the building.

Below: The resulting core would enable him to give us some accurate dates for the timbers.

original building. From the church roof Stewart and Peter could see the potential angle of attack, and Robin had located references to a sconce (a small earthwork) 137 metres (150 yards) – a musket-shot length – from High Ercall Hall.

Mick now had a chance to see some possible models of the mansion we were looking for on a ground plan. Richard had suggested two types. One was based on Apsley Castle, which he felt might be not quite grand enough, and the other, appropriately enough, on Aston Hall. Both were from approximately the same time as High Ercall and were relatively local. Mick was amazed that the plan for Aston Hall fitted into High Ercall's garden and that it, too, had colonnaded arches.

Somewhere at a secret firing range approved by the Ministry of Defence Phil was testing the technology that would have been used to destroy High Ercall. After months of negotiations and licence agreements Ella Galinski had

Below: The Civil War gets nearer. Stewart examines the damage from a pistol shot.

Opposite: Jenni in her 'you can't dig this yet I haven't drawn it' position.

Tony indicating the presence of the necessary digits to fire a bow.

obtained permission to fire a live cannon as the programme's cameo (see pages 124–125). The explosion was awesome – like a physical shock – and was followed by a wave of smoke that billowed and hid the target: the gabions. A direct hit on both was finally achieved and Phil and the re-enactor were able to see that a 2-pound shot did not penetrate them. One wonders, however, what a larger cannonball would do.

Before lunch I asked the director, Michael 'Dougie' Douglas, whether he cared that we hadn't found the wall on the south side of the house. He replied pragmatically that he wasn't too concerned because there was already a lot going on that worked for the programme. However, I felt a nagging discontent and, coincidentally, at that point Tony asked me if we'd lost a bit of 'edge' on this final day. We spent a while talking this over and I said I was concerned because I didn't want Day Three to be too self-satisfied – there were still targets we hadn't reached.

My inclination was to shake things up and I talked to Jenni about opening a large, final trench across the lawn to see if a last try could find the missing wall – the one that had borne the brunt of the Parliamentary attack. She voiced a number of practical concerns – we didn't have enough polythene ... we'd make a mess of the lawn (it already looked like the Somme!) – but I felt that she didn't really need to bother about issues like these. On a *Time Team* dig we should all concentrate on finding the archaeological answer and anything else can be sorted out. Her sensitivity seemed laudable on one level, but it was rather like talking to a climber who has lost sight of the summit in order to make the base camp neat and tidy.

Jenni and I had a heart-to-heart talk and, although she still expressed concern, she agreed to go for the final trench. We had a few hours of the day left, it was raining and we hadn't yet got Peter's agreement to savage yet more of his lawn. The diggers were exhausted and many of them had blisters after

Phil conducting a close examination of the interior of his hat.

three hard days. I grabbed John Gater, who had been 'geofizzing' the grounds throughout the three-day dig, and told him what was needed – a quick radar transect – and that he had twenty minutes to do a job that normally takes three hours. Ian Powlesland was dispatched to crank up the mini-digger and Melinda Smith was sent to chat the owner up.

With the rain belting down, John and his geophysics team went for it and, with diggers running in all directions to get spades and Ian revving up the mini-digger, the final trench went in. After two or three scrapes of the digger bucket we heard the gratifying sound of stone. Further excavation in the final hour produced pieces of seventeenth-century glass and a substantial wall made of high-quality stone. We'd found it. This was the wall nearest to the Parliamentarian attack.

Sitting in the cab of the mini-digger I wrote the final piece to camera, adding the new information while our researcher Ishbel Macdonald dug out

Below: Filling in the background history, Mick and Tony talking to Peter Bennett. On the left, the director Michael Douglas, is trying to remember the plot.

Opposite: Phil delicately traversing the archaeology in his size-ten boots.

critical facts. We had found the crucial wall and I described the glass as being potentially what the Royalists looked through as the final attack against them was mounted. After three days of exhausting work everyone in the team had pitched in to find this last piece of the jigsaw, and the television crews had been able to record everything that happened. We had pushed for that final effort and, because we made the effort, the gods of excavation shone on us and we found the wall.

In February 1646 the Royalists went too far – they attacked a local fair and robbed and looted what they could. It was now time for the Parliamentarians to act. They erected earthworks like the sconce we had found to give them a major advantage and cannonballs were brought to High Ercall. At the end of March a nine-hour bombardment took place and destroyed the southern side of the building, one remnant of which – the wall – we had managed to find. The end was near and the Royalists asked for terms. They surrendered and 212 men and 40 officers walked out of High Ercall with their weapons.

Because of what everyone had achieved I was able to write this final piece to camera with a sense of well-being, and although it may have been a touch purple – 'media tart' said Tony – we knew it would work. In those circumstances I wasn't too ashamed to have waxed a bit lyrical. As I wrote it, I could almost hear cannons firing somewhere in the distance and Phil letting fly at Civil War defences – and I felt that *Time Team* had won its own small battle in the trenches of High Ercall!

It would be a strange coincidence, but I wondered if any of the shot fired at High Ercall had been made in the furnace under what is now the Kynnersley Arms at Leighton, also in Shropshire.

With all the efforts people had made in the last hours, it was nice that we were able to produce a great final piece to camera which Tony did real justice despite his earlier comment. This was one of the pieces to camera that gave me a shiver when I heard it delivered by Tony: 'We've seen the force of the muskets and cannons that were trained on this place. It was pounded by countless rounds during three bloody sieges. Over a thousand men were killed or wounded, and yet amazingly we found traces of the structure they sheltered behind still surviving. Our last trench hit the wall that was the part of the building near the action. Maybe this glass [holds up fragment] was still in place when they looked out to see the Parliamentarians advancing. Over the last three days High Ercall has revealed a new chapter in its history. The story and the evidence of a much bloodier past.'

Victor Ambrus, our artist in residence, displays one of his prized possessions. He decided to put it on once he saw the accuracy of Phil's musket fire.

ELLA'S CAMEO:
CIVIL WAR GABIONS AND LIVE CANNONS

After working on so many *Time Team* programmes it can be difficult to think of new ideas for the cameo sequences. I was really pleased when one of the team suggested gabions. These are huge drums made from woven wythies – preferably hazel – which were filled with earth to form a barricade against gun and cannon fire (rather like massive sandbags). We sourced some lovely seventeenth-century illustrations, courtesy of the Royal Armouries at Fort Nelson near Portsmouth, and I learnt that gabions and wickerwork were still being used as retaining walls for trenches in the First World War as they were one of the lightest and safest ways of containing earth and giving protection from artillery. The basketwork doesn't cause as much damage as metal when it splinters and the earth absorbs the impact of shells.

Below: The two gabions being completed. Both proved to be highly effective.

I thought we ought to finish the experiment properly by firing a cannon ball into the gabions to test their effectiveness. If I could have foreseen the can of worms I was about to open, I would have put the idea to one side.

I found a willing group of re-enactors with a half-sized replica saker (an early form of cannon) and appropriate firearms and black powder licences; a foundry at Blist's Hill that could make the right size cannon balls (there isn't much call for the manufacture of these nowadays); and an MOD-approved firing range with a suitable backdrop of a 30 metre (100 feet) cliff face. I thought I was doing really well – but my problems were only just starting.

The trouble was that nobody normally tries to fire live cannons. They don't need to – these weapons make a spectacular show using blanks – so I'd hit a really grey legal area. No one wanted to commit themselves, and I certainly didn't want to break the law or put anyone in danger. The use of live firearms is necessarily highly controlled in Britain, but everything would have been OK if the calibre of the cannon had been under 2 inches. Ours was just over and that caused a lot of consternation among the police, the MOD, various over-zealous members of artillery societies and even contacts in the Home Office. I ended up with a mass of conflicting advice and only a matter of days to sort everything out. Luckily, I had Ron Curley on my side. A gunsmith who has made and proofed many guns and cannons, he was willing to act as safety officer and guide me through the red tape.

Yet another problem was that the cannon had to be proofed to fire ammunition safely. Like most cannons in re-enactments, it had only ever been used to fire blanks before. Proofing entailed chaining the cannon down and firing about three pounds of lead shot, using a much greater amount of powder than we would need to use in the cameo – about six pounds – into 6 metres (20 feet) of sand in a test shed at the Birmingham Proof House. It was all very last-minute and thankfully the cannon passed the test without the barrel being destroyed, but it still hadn't fired a solid ball …

When we finally managed to fire the cannon at our gabions the atmosphere was electric because nobody knew how it would react. We had visions of it leaping into the air with the force of the explosion, and shearing off the bolts that fastened it to the gun carriage. No one was allowed anywhere near the cannon once the fuse was lit in case it exploded. We only used half a pound of black powder, again for safety reasons, but Ron said that was enough to send the ball up to a mile away. He estimated that it would have been travelling at between 600 and 800 mph when it hit our gabion from the close range of 25 metres (27 yards) – and that it did the same amount of damage as a larger ball, fired with several pounds of powder from several hundred yards away, would have done.

Top: Ella Galinski with executive producer Phil Clarke looking through old diagrams and drawings of gabions.

Bottom: One of many firings, the noise of which was stupendous. At point-blank range the cannon proved to be accurate enough to hit the gabion, although this first shot, which can be seen 'splashing' into the bank, was rather high.

As we dug at Cheshunt Park, we began to uncover evidence of the earlier excavations.

Cheshunt Park
Hertfordshire

'Are we standing on top of an undiscovered town?'

Tony Robinson's piece to camera: 'Forty years ago some amateur archaeologists discovered [he holds up a complete roof tile] a wealth of Roman finds in this park at Cheshunt in Hertfordshire. The archaeologists were told to keep quiet about their discovery because the British Museum thought what they'd found might be very important … A huge hoard of Roman coins had even been discovered in the area at the turn of the century [Tony approaches boxes and boxes of finds]. But their boxes of Roman brick, tile and pottery, together with their detailed records, have been sitting, ignored, in a local museum ever since. Somewhere close by ran Ermine Street, the main link to the Roman Empire's most northerly stronghold at York. Where I am now should be about a day's march from London, so are we standing on top of an undiscovered town, a military marching post or just a Roman Little Chef? *Time Team* have three days to work out what these important finds are really telling us. Join us as we try to unravel the mystery of Cheshunt Park.'

Roman Roads and Roadside Settlements

Roads in the Roman Empire had several main functions: to allow the army to move swiftly and easily; to encourage free movement of goods for trading purposes by joining up the network of towns and forts; and to 'open up' previously unexploited or underdeveloped areas bringing *romanitas*, the way of life that defined what it was to be a part of the empire, to newly won lands and their inhabitants. But Roman roads may also have had far more abstract and subtle purposes: archaeologist Robert Witcher suggested recently that they could be used to manipulate the everyday world and experience of their subjects. For example, building roads that deliberately avoided old, tribal centres of power would challenge and deny peoples' memories of these places.

There is one fact that everyone knows about Roman roads: they are always dead straight. But this is not strictly true. Rather, they usually consist of a series of short, straight sections aligned in one direction. The surveyors were highly sensitive to the constraints imposed by natural terrain, and would readily deviate from a straight line where necessary, usually when there were major landscape obstacles such as rivers or hills. None the less, the accuracy of the surveying is sometimes incredible. One expert has pointed out that, 'the Fosse Way runs for over 200 miles yet is never more than 8 miles from the direct line between Axminster and Lincoln'.

Many towns either grew up, or were established from the outset, at major road junctions. Some small roadside ones were clearly 'official' foundations, placed deliberately at a specific location to fulfil a specific purpose. One example of this was probably Tripontium ('Three Bridges'), which straddles Watling Street (the A5) in Warwickshire, north-east of Rugby, and which is mentioned in an early third-century list of British posting stations. Buildings called mansiones, the official inns or hotels where members of the imperial post service could change horses and rest, are characteristic of these stations. Excavations at Tripontium have uncovered the mansio, which underwent several phases of building but which included a large and complex suite of

heated baths. Although only a relatively small staging post, Tripontium clearly had other pretensions and the excavators noted that the baths are, 'much larger than … the normal villa baths, or indeed the sort of baths that would be attached to a mansio.'

But roads generally also acted as magnets for less formal settlements, usually because of the trading potential they offered, and as well as the 'nodal' and imperial planted towns, settlements tended to grow in an 'organic' way along stretches of road. It is clear that from small beginnings many of these could have become large enough to be classed as towns in their own right. The larger roadside settlements like Shepton, Mancetter in Warwickshire and Wall in Staffordshire fall into a classification archaeologists call 'middle order settlements' – that is, they are halfway between the major towns and cities and smaller rural sites. It is looking increasingly likely that we can expect more such sites to be discovered, filling in settlement 'gaps' along Britain's major Roman roads.

I have a very strong image in my mind when I think of this dig – an image which stayed with me for some time after we had completed our work there. It was of our 'punter', Jean Mullinger, standing by our final trench on the last day of excavation. She was looking down at what we'd unearthed on the site that she, her friends and family had always thought was important, and which had largely been ignored by the powers that be. She stood contemplating what was in the trench with an air of quiet satisfaction. It was at this point that I really felt pleased we'd decided to do that particular dig.

In the 1960s, Jean Mullinger and her husband Tom had begun to do some trial excavations in a field at Cheshunt Park. They had taken an amateur interest in archaeology and were drawn to the site's proximity to one of Roman Britain's main roads, Ermine Street, the link between London and York. Cheshunt is also the point where Roman soldiers may have camped or taken a break on their way to the north as it is approximately one day's march out of London.

Below: Somewhere, out there in the distance, there had to be a Roman road. But exactly where did it cross this field?

Opposite: We constantly had to refer to maps and records to try and locate the route of the road.

Jean and Tom were joined by groups of friends and their children and started to uncover a lot of Roman material, including coarse wares – pottery used for everyday domestic use – metalwork, glass and roof tiles, all within an area that could have been adjacent to Ermine Street. They kept a record of their work detailing their finds meticulously and, when they had a large amount of evidence of Roman activity, took this to the British Museum. Here Jean was given the impression that she should probably keep quiet about her finds. Although one or two eminent Romanists took an interest in the site and visited Jean's dig from time to time, no professional archaeologists could be persuaded to pursue her work at the site.

The considerable archive of material the Mullingers and their friends had amassed over the years they worked on the site included an excellent set of trench records, with drawings and sections. Few archaeologists had taken much interest in these, but when Jenni Butterworth began to look at them as

Behind the crew and assembled archaeologists are the woods that had grown a great deal since the earlier excavations.

we did our preliminary research into the site she became increasingly enthusiastic about the efforts the Mullingers had made despite the lack of enthusiasm from the authorities. Although many of the drawings are not in a conventional archaeological format, they are real works of art and show that a dedicated amateur group can create a superb record of its work. They gave us most of the key facts, and the existence of this archive material, and my feeling that here was a group of people whom *Time Team* should be supporting, made me keen to do a dig on the site.

With the exception of St Albans, there aren't many Roman sites in Hertfordshire and we had an encouraging response from Stewart Bryant, the local county archaeological officer, who felt that something ought to be done to resolve the questions the Mullingers had raised. Had they discovered a roadside settlement, a fort where soldiers rested after their first day's march from London or a stopping-place where the men could obtain food and drink

Jenni and Carenza had to work out where exactly the edge of the wood had been in Jean Mullinger's time.

– the Roman equivalent of a service station? Some of the Mullingers' finds – for example, the odd piece of metalworking slag – suggested industrial activity on the site, or possibly even a small roadside shrine. Other local finds from the area surrounding the site included a pig-lead ingot which our local Roman expert, Ros Niblett, believed could indicate a trading post. Jean had also unearthed some pieces of tile that could be tesserae, but these had since been lost. Tesserae and the roof tiles might indicate the presence of a villa near the road.

There had been unconfirmed reports that a hoard of over 280 coins, including ones from the reigns of the emperors Gallienus and Gratian in the third and fourth centuries, had been found in 1904. This made us wonder if the authorities' reaction to the Mullingers' finds could be connected to the fact that they thought there might be an important site at Cheshunt but weren't keen to publicise the fact in case it was plundered by less scrupulous amateurs.

Opposite: Phil, in his lumberjack shirt, prepares to tackle the woodland.

Above: Jenni, with part of Jean Mullinger's archive report, working out where exactly we had to put a trench.

Below: Removing turf for a new trench. This can often be one of the toughest bits of work, particularly when the soil has been baked by the sun.

Opposite: A rare shot of Jack Holmes, long-serving Time Team camera assistant.

The name Cheshunt could combine two Latin words – *caestra* and *funta* – and according to Guy de la Bédoyère, our Roman expert who took an initial look at the finds before we started excavating, could imply that there had been a walled settlement (*caestra*) by a spring or stream (*funta*), or by an elaborately built well or basin.

On Day One our first trenches were opened in Pump Field, which is adjacent to the possible route of the road and the site of the Mullingers' main trial excavations. They had located a stone channel that they thought could be part of a hypocaust system – for underfloor heating – in this area and we needed to confirm that this was what they had found and see if it was part of a villa or had some other function. Opening Trench One on the previous excavation would give the geophysics team a chance to survey the rest of the field while we were doing so, and would also provide our diggers with a quick way of testing the extent to which we could use the Jean Mullingers' plans as a guide to the site.

Locating exactly where we were on the site was made more difficult by the fact that key landmarks had disappeared or become overgrown or removed. In the days before global positioning systems and electronic surveying techniques it was logical to relate trenches to specific landmarks. In the case of Pump Field the Mullingers had used a metal fence, a telegraph pole and lines of trees, all of which had undergone many changes since the excavations were recorded. After a lot of thrashing about in the undergrowth we managed to find the fence, and the remains of a post hole which enabled us to locate where the telegraph pole had been.

Talking to Henry Chapman later he explained what a unique challenge the dig had been to him. It was his job to correlate a mixture of various excavation plans and Jean Mullinger's memories of the site. We were particularly interested in a series of depressions in the field which may have been related to the previous

Opposite: Endless communications – Mick and I keep in touch with progress in the trenches.

Above: Phil in action doing a bit of forest clearance. Somewhere in there is a fence and the remains of a telegraph pole.

It was great to be able to show Jean Mullinger what we had found.

excavations. In a nice example of 'survey speak' he described finding the fence and telegraph pole as having achieved 'a level of survey control'.

Henry also had to try to track the Roman road, this time by combining evidence from work done previously both to the north and the south of the Pump Field. The problem was that there was a gap of several hundred metres between the known points on the road, so any slight inaccuracy in the projected angle of the road would be exaggerated in the area of the Pump Field in between, where we were trying to locate the road. It may come as a surprise to many of us who rely on maps that the position of a road on a modern map may not be correct. For archaeologists, often the only way to find the accurate position is to re-excavate.

Extra tree and bramble growth had begun to cover the boundaries of the original park since the 1960s. Jean was on hand to give us an approximate idea of where they might have been, but we needed good evidence from trenches to be sure we were in the right place as memory can play amazing tricks on us all. Predicting the road's actual route was equally tricky. A lot of poring over maps before the shoot had produced two contrasting ideas: one, that the road had cut through the site in a straight line; the other, that the area had been swampy which might have required it to deviate to the west.

Time Team has hunted for Roman roads before and it is often a frustrating business. People have a classical image of these roads, that involves large blocks of stone, neatly combined with deep ditches on either side, and all laid on gravel and hard core that appears in a section when you excavate it. This is rarely the case. The stone was valuable and robbed out for local buildings, and a once straight route can turn into a series of muddy tracks as the road deteriorates.

Phil Harding opened Trench One near the hollow in the Pump Field and decided to test the straight-line theory by putting Katie Hirst's trench –

Phil and Gary, one of our diggers, dig the dirt.

Trench Two – across the possible route of the road, based on the lie of the land and aerial photographs showing a distinct linear feature and crop marks. Trench Three was located in the parkland to the north of the remains of a stately home. This had overlooked the site until it had been demolished in the 1970s and was only 20 metres (22 yards) from the Mullingers' excavations. As Stewart Ainsworth pointed out, its landscaped gardens might have obscured the evidence of the road. The sheer scale of the earthworks gardens like these create is often hard to believe. Archaeology can be hidden under tons of earth and the problem is exacerbated by the planting of large specimen trees.

By the end of Day One Phil had managed to locate some of the features described by the Mullingers in Trench One, but Trench Two, across the possible road, had produced a rather ill-defined ditch and a mass of gravel. Guy pointed out that we could be underestimating the width of the road, which might be

In some cases we were finding pots that were almost intact in one area of the trench.

7–10 metres (23–33 feet), and we decided to extend the trench on the following day to see if we could locate the ditches that usually survive on either side of the roads the Romans built.

On Day Two we asked one of *Time Team*'s regular experts, Peter Reynolds from the Iron Age village at Butser Ancient Farm, to look at the stone structure that Phil was uncovering in Trench One. Pete thought the stone-lined, drain-like feature was possibly part of an oven used for malting or drying barley and not the remains of a hypocaust system. This suggested the rather pleasant possibility, from Phil's point of view, that we had the remains of a brewing house that had provided thirsty Roman soldiers with ale.

After overnight discussions with Mick and the director Lawrence Vuillamy, I felt we needed to get nearer to the possible line of the road. In theory, any wayside service establishment – and the malting or barley-drying feature certainly suggested that we might find the remains of a Roman tavern – would have opened on to the roadside so that

Carenza taking advantage of Guy de la Bédoyère's vast experience of Roman artefacts, to identify some of our finds.

143

goods and services could be sold to passing customers. We all thought that the nearer we could get to the road, the better the archaeology ought to become and Trench Four was opened up between Trench One and the potential line of the road. Jenni got stuck into it with Carenza Lewis and fairly soon it produced some pieces of Roman pottery.

As we still weren't sure whether or not Ermine Street had changed track across the landscape to avoid a swamp, Mick and Stewart went up in the helicopter to follow its known route and see how it might cross the site. There appeared to be some earthworks in the area and after landing Stewart was able to locate these and gave us a position for another trench. I felt we had to bite the bullet and should be willing to cross the line of the road anywhere we felt there was a good archaeological or topographical reason for doing so, and Trench Five duly went in. The number of trenches we were opening was becoming a bit unnerving, and I had a worrying image of *Time Team* cutting a large number of slit trenches across Hertfordshire, all of which would hit vague ditches and the usual rather uninspiring gravel. However, by the end of Day Two, Trench Five, the second

Opposite: Mick tries to work out how much top soil could have been piled on the road.

Below: Phil pointing out the likely level of the Roman road.

trench across the line of the road, appeared to have a more substantial ditch to encourage us and Phil was ready to make a determined effort to sort it out the following day.

On Day Two we had been joined by a group of surveyors who were going to introduce Stewart and Henry to the fine art of Roman surveying. Lawrence and Ella Galinski had had the great idea of pitting modern and ancient survey methods against each other for our cameo (see pages 154–155).

At the start of Day Three I felt we needed to go for broke in the woodland area next to Pump Field. It was between the Mullingers' excavation and the road, but the presence of masses of trees and undergrowth had initially made us a bit reluctant to venture too far into it. With Ian Powlesland and Jenni, I searched for a route through the woods that would allow us to dig a long trench that would stand a chance of cutting through the line of the road somewhere.

Carenza and Tony both excited by the mosaic.

It's very useful having someone like Ian around. Not only is he a highly qualified archaeologist with a particular knowledge of prehistoric pottery, but he is also a skilled driver of the mini-digger. This is invaluable at sites where access might be difficult. At Cheshunt we needed to find a route through the small trees that wouldn't damage their roots. Where there are many trees we use the size of the canopy as rough guide to how far the roots are likely to spread. The mini-digger was particularly useful at Cheshunt because the soil had been compacted by two small paths but Ian's experience with using it gave me confidence that he would be able to cut down layer by layer at least until any archaeology was exposed.

Around mid-morning Phil at last found some Roman pottery in Trench Five's ditch, and the extension of Katie Hirst's trench – Trench Two – had revealed ditches that were the best evidence yet for the Roman road. Could we find where Ermine Street was in relation to the Mullingers' site and would this

Above: Ian's work with the mini digger turned out to be particularly effective on this dig, because he could work between the trees.

Overleaf: Roman structures at last! Kate Edwards lays out scales prior to taking photographs for the post-ex report.

147

The Problems of Post-excavation

The final day of excavation at Cheshunt Park saw a final trench being opened in the search for evidence of occupation along what we now knew to be the route of Ermine Street, the primary Roman road from London to York. Trenches opened during excavations in the 1960s had revealed intriguing structures and evidence of industry along the roadside.

At the eleventh hour, excavators in Trench Nine revealed a large, if somewhat battered, mosaic floor. It was probably the surface of a courtyard and was exactly the sort of find we needed to confirm that there had been domestic occupation at this staging post alongside the road. It was made from 2.5-centimetre (1-inch) square pieces of cut tile bedded on to compacted earth. There was no bonding material or decoration and, although some tesserae had mortar on their undersides, it was clear that materials that were to hand had been reused to create the mosaic.

To have a full record of a trench a written, photographic and drawn record has to be completed. Recording a mosaic floor with over 700 tesserae in a very short time means that a creative alternative has to be found. We decided that a large sheet of plastic and a permanent-marker pen would allow us to generate a very accurate, if oversized, record of the mosaic at a scale of 1:1.

In order to include the illustration in reports and publications the unwieldy piece of plastic had to be reduced to a practical size and digitised. After much industrious photocopying – we found a copier that wouldn't melt the plastic – and cutting and pasting, we finally ended up with a scaled-down version of our mosaic.

reveal more archaeology? With Jean and her family visiting, we made a final push and Ian located two areas in the woodland where we could cut a trench – Trench Six – that would take us from the area of the original excavations and across the potential site of the road.

In Trench One we had now discovered a hardened stone-covered area of floor next to what Peter had thought was a drying oven and Jenni and Carenza were finding large amounts of Roman pottery in Trench Four. In Trench Five Phil was able to confirm that we had a large and substantial ditch

Above: Preparing the
final trench and its
mosaic to show to Jean
Mullinger.

with Roman pottery. According to Stewart, this linked up to the aerial photographs of crop marks and the earthworks he and Mick had seen from the helicopter. With only hours to go Ian contacted me and said he thought I should 'come and have a look' in his trench. The more understated this kind of request is on the final day, the more excited I become. When I arrived at the trench I was not disappointed: he'd found an area of mosaic flooring! It wasn't anything fancy – just good old terracotta-coloured tiles – but it was mosaic and definitely Roman and suggested a sophisticated building fronting on to the road. Both Lawrence and I breathed a sigh of relief.

Jean and her family were delighted when, in the final hour of the dig, we were able to show them what we had found. The proximity of the road, indicated by the ditches located in Trenches Two and Five, added to the importance of the site and the mosaic pavement confirmed that there had been an important Roman building there. Mick and Pete took the view that it

Above: Phil receives his due reward for a hard day's work, possibly in the same location as a Roman soldier would have enjoyed a cup of wine.

Opposite: Phil posing for a potential shampoo advertisement.

may well have been a wayside establishment that sold beer and food to passing soldiers and had its own brewing facilities at the rear.

Time and time again, it is Victor Ambrus's drawings that the viewers most want to see and Cheshunt was no exception. When sites are in public places – as so many this year were – as soon as Victor appears he is surrounded by a group of people anxious to see 'what it looked like'. His drawings are usually full of energy and life, and the inclusion of figures gives us a sense of proportion. They form an accessible route into what the past might have looked like. Inevitably there is an element of conjecture, but most people are able to accept this and enjoy the delight of being transported back in time.

After all those years *Time Team* had been able to confirm the Mullingers' belief that this was an important piece of archaeology, one that will add a new Roman site to the maps of Hertfordshire.

THE CAMEO⊙:
A ROMAN SURVEY

Cheshunt presented certain unique survey challenges that required a wide range of modern techniques including the use of a global positioning system (GPS) and an electronic theodolite and distance measurer (EDM) in addition to the more conventional tapes and compass. We decided, therefore, that we would base the cameo on a surveying theme and compare the effectiveness of modern approaches with those used during the Roman period. On the one side we had Henry and his modern equipment and on the other two representatives of the Roman army with Roman surveying gear. We obviously couldn't have the Romans surveying their own remains, so the two sides were asked to compete to lay out an ancient marching camp.

The cameo presented its own set of challenges. Each side had to lay out half of the outline of the camp, including corners, roads and the locations of internal features like the main tents. This is the kind of preliminary surveying the Romans would have had to do before ditches were cut and fences were constructed. Once the lines were laid out the results were to be marked by mowing the grass into the shape of the camp.

Below: The legionnaires were on hand to protect their surveyors.

Opposite: Modern technology versus a Roman surveying staff. Each are dressed appropriately.

The GPS was set against a reconstructed Roman groma, a stout staff with a wooden cross positioned on top of it. Weighted strings hung from the arms of the cross which were lined up together to provide right angles. Using the groma and other pieces of reconstructed Roman survey equipment the two re-enactors set to work on one half of the camp whilst Henry worked on the other half using the GPS. The results were not unexpected. The hi-tech modern methods were much more efficient – Henry completed the job in approximately half an hour while the two surveyors took nearly four hours just to set out the perimeter. However, the accuracy of the Roman methods were not what we might have expected. In Henry's words, 'It was with some surprise that I realised that the accuracy provided by the Roman methods was extremely precise and would be quite acceptable within today's survey requirements.'

Carl Thorp from the Cornwall Archaeological Unit
was on hand at Gear Farm and Caer Vallack to
help identify any prehistoric pottery finds.

'HOW MUCH CAN TIME TEAM FIND OUT ABOUT THESE TWO HILL FORTS IN JUST THREE DAYS?'

Tony Robinson's piece to camera: 'This massive field is part of one of Cornwall's most impressive hill forts. You can see the shape of it on this aerial photo [holds up photograph] – a huge 18-acre field surrounded by a big bank and ditch. It's so big that an antiquarian visiting this site at Gear in 1916 suggested it might be an Iron Age city. Very little, in fact, is known about it and even less is known about this [he points to Caer Vallack on the photograph], a smaller hill fort which overlooks it. This one, as you can see, has two enclosures [he points to trees on the horizon] and it's literally just next door.'

Tony at Caer Vallack: 'This is Caer Vallack and when the same antiquarian, Charles Henderson, visited here he wondered if this "fortress", as he called it, was where the Iron Age people had fled to when under attack. The trouble is that although these are two of Cornwall's most important prehistoric sites, very little is known about them. No one even knows if these two sites existed at the same time. Which is why *Time Team* are here. We've been given the rare chance to find out if they do belong to the same period and what was going on inside them over 2,000 years ago. It's a big challenge, but how much can *Time Team* find out about these two hill forts in just three days?'

The Iron Age

The hill forts of the Iron Age period in Britain represent some of the country's best-known and most spectacular surviving ancient monuments. However, the term 'hill fort' sometimes tends to be used indiscriminately, and can be applied to a whole range of different types of site. The smaller of these can be grouped into a more general class known as 'hill top enclosures', usually because they are less strongly fortified than forts.

There is a clear regional variation in the distribution of hill forts. They are densely concentrated in the west (west Wales, Devon and Cornwall, the Welsh borders, Somerset, Dorset, Hampshire, Wiltshire), and become increasingly sparse towards the east. Interestingly, this distribution mirrors the size of the forts. The smaller sites, those of 1.2 hectares (3 acres) or less, are overwhelmingly found in the far west. Medium (about 1.2–6 hectares/3–15 acres) and larger forts are found mainly in the Welsh borders and central southern England. Not all hill forts would have been occupied simultaneously, and we have reliable dating evidence from only a tiny minority of all the known forts. It is also necessary to remember that many sites were occupied long before the Iron Age and reveal highly complex sequences of development. The forts themselves may represent merely the culmination of generations of activity.

Certainly some of the larger hill forts are vast: Maiden Castle in Dorset runs to 19 hectares (47 acres) in its final phase. Even larger is Ham Hill in Somerset which, at 84 hectares (210 acres), is the largest hill fort of its type in Britain. There was activity at Maiden Castle from at least the early Neolithic period, including the construction of a large causewayed enclosure. Bronze Age pottery and possible structures indicate occupation by the first metal-using peoples. In its early Iron Age phase (about the middle of the fourth century BC) only the eastern end of the ridge was enclosed. Subsequent development westwards meant that by the early first century BC the site had reached its maximum size and boasted arguably the most impressive and sophisticated system of ditched ramparts anywhere in Britain.

Because of their size and impressiveness, hill forts they have until quite recently dominated Iron Age archaeology, but in fact they totally distort our view of the way most Iron Age people actually lived. Just as we know now that most medieval rural peasants did not live in nucleated villages, we also know that the overwhelming majority of Iron Age folk did not live in hill forts. The so-called Iron Age lake villages near Glastonbury in Somerset, excavated between 1892 and 1917, represent the first serious archaeological investigation into non-hill fort rural settlements that reached anything approaching modern standards. These villages, in their sheer range and wealth of finds, much of it organic material preserved by the waterlogged conditions, are exceptional. However, since the Second World War archaeologists have come to realise, mainly through aerial photography, that the Iron Age landscape of southern England was densely packed with farmsteads and small settlements, a fact noted over 2,000 years ago by Julius Caesar on his push northwards through Kent.

We have realised that it is not enough just to study individual sites like hill forts. A reasonable appreciation of the way communities lived comes only through looking at entire landscapes. In the Iron Age, as in other periods, we are beginning at last to understand the importance of trying to restore the overwhelming majority of ordinary people to the landscapes which they knew.

igging in prehistory is always a bit of a risk. Evidence of the past in a period like the Iron Age can be difficult to interpret and at sites like Gear, a huge earthwork surrounding a 7 hectare (18 acre) field, there is often a contrast between their size and the relatively limited evidence of their occupation.

I had been attracted to Gear because little was known about what is one of the largest earthworks in Cornwall. We'd had meetings with Ian Morrison, the English Heritage inspector, and his positive response proved to be another encouraging factor. There comes a point in a monument's life when all the theorising has to be replaced by excavation and this would be a research-evaluation dig that might help to illuminate a period of history about which little is known.

The Lizard – the most southern peninsula of Cornwall – is a unique and beautiful landscape which has escaped the more extreme effects of incoming

In some areas the preservation was fantastic. The further down the slope, the deeper the soil cover and the clearer the Iron Age remains.

cultures and later development. There are signs that the area was left relatively untouched by the post-Iron-Age influences of the Romans and Saxons, and today it is still possible to see traces of Bronze Age field systems. I'd first come across the site by chance when I'd stopped off during a driving holiday to buy a selection of the excellent organic fruit and veg grown at Gear Farm. A chance discussion with Rex Hosking had led to him showing me objects he'd picked up over many years after the main 7 hectare (18 acre) field at Gear had been ploughed.

In Rex and his wife Pat we had two 'punters' who cared about the archaeology and wanted to look after it by adjusting the way they farmed and managed the site. It is often farmers who are the first to spot the archaeology and who ultimately have to care for it. They often don't tell local archaeologists about important finds because they are worried that their ability to farm the site will be adversely affected. However, with many of them looking to

We had fairly quickly begun to see features and Phil was working away at the evidence delicately with his dental pick.

diversify, an archaeological site can be an important visitor attraction and English Heritage are keen to show that farmers and archaeologists can work together in a way that preserves sites but doesn't restrict the need for every farmer to make as much return from their fields as possible. It is often a case of simply restricting the ploughing to a shallower depth, or selecting certain key areas of archaeology and managing these more carefully. In the case of Gear Farm, English Heritage were keen to look at a site where this positive aspect of farmers' guardianship of sites could be presented.

Gear Farm is in the process of becoming fully organic and is diversifying into selling not only fruit and vegetables but also locally sourced fish and meat. The interesting aspect of organic farming is that it is not always totally positive from an archaeological point of view because fields may be rotated more regularly on organic farms than on non-organic ones.

One of the best aspects of the dig was that at last we were able to get on to some real farmland after all the traumas of foot-and-mouth. Luckily Cornwall had remained free of the disease and we had carefully liased with both Rex and his nephew Andrew Hosking, owner of Caer Vallack, the second site we were excavating, to ensure they had no concerns about us filming. It was particularly encouraging that Andrew seemed to have a real fascination with Caer Vallack, and had always thought it was an important site.

Caer Vallack is a fascinating round about 1.5 kilometres (1 mile) from Gear Farm. A round is a Cornish feature, a prehistoric, circular bank and ditch, enclosing a settlement. One of the key elements of the research design was to see if the two locations were contemporary. The research design had been written by Jenni Butterworth and Pete Herring, senior archaeologist at Cornwall Archaeological Unit, after discussions with Ian Morrison. As both sites were scheduled we had to produce a highly detailed scheme of work for English Heritage and the government to approve. We would also need a licence to excavate or do any geophysics surveys, and the digs would be closely monitored. The licence specifies such details as who is working on a site and their qualifications, how an excavation will be recorded and what experts will be consulted.

I had been keen to get Rex's finds examined by an expert before we began the dig, and had taken them to Carl Thorpe at the Cornwall Archaeological Unit. Carl had worked with *Time Team* before at Launceston and came highly recommended. His report went into detail about all the objects Rex had found, which included flints, pottery and an interesting fragment of a stone bowl. The most tantalising revelation was his view that the pottery showed 'extensive' settlement in the Iron Age.

The large number of finds made us keen to incorporate a fieldwalking element in the dig, taking advantage of a part of the site Rex had ploughed up in order to try out a new organic crop. Teresa Hall, a researcher who had worked with Mick Aston before at Chatwick in Somerset, was roped in to coordinate the gridding out of the area into 10 metre (33 feet) squares and local archaeology students and volunteers were brought in to walk them. Our aim was to identify the artefacts that were found by the fieldwalkers and see if there was a significant scatter that indicated particular activity in a specific area. Rex had already been finding large amounts of slag at Gear. Was this evidence of industrial activity on the site or had it been brought in to cultivate the land   at one time farmers had used slag waste to improve the texture of heavy soils?

Phil begins the fieldwalk. The canes carefully marked out the gridded areas.

At the start of Day One the fieldwalkers were out in force at Gear and we would be opening four trenches: two at Gear and two at Caer Vallack. The latter were already under way. Our aim was to section the ditch and bank earthworks on both sites to try to find out if there was any dating evidence in the ditches. Would they show that the two sites were linked in some way?

Graham Dixon, the director, and I had discussed the double nature of the programme at an early stage in the project. Having two locations is not ideal, as everyone's time is divided, but I felt it was important to see if they were linked and English Heritage were keen to resolve this issue. The problem for the director is that he can't be in two places at once and on Day One this created a classic piece of *Time Team* tension.

Graham was directing Tony's opening piece to camera at Caer Vallack early in the morning and it was taking a long time. Tony had spent the previous day in the midst of political tension at meetings with the government and had had a five-hour drive to reach us. This was having its effect and his opening piece needed a lot of takes. Meanwhile at Gear we had cameras, a crew and good geophysics – and it was important for us to start on the trenches in the main

Below: Joe Ellison supervises the helicopter, which would give us an amazing view of the farm from the air. In the background are the Royal Navy 'Sea Kings' which were also flying that day.

field area. As *Time Team* had worked on Iron Age sites before I knew how complicated they could be, and didn't want to lose two hours on the first day then regret this on Day Three.

However, directors can often get stuck in a mindset that requires certain steps to be taken before a trench is dug: the geophysics team must be shown at work, a discussion of the results and *Time Team*'s strategy has to be filmed, and another scene has to show the trench being sprayed with coloured liner and the turf coming off. Only then are we allowed to take the soil off! All this can take ages and, in order to get the archaeology under way, I often try to persuade the director to film a trench retrospectively, after it has been opened, and add the explanations after we have started. This can produce tensions and on Day One at Gear, with everyone suffering from PET (Pre-Excavation Tension) Graham, who had started at Caer Vallack, was coming out with a series of comments like 'How's your film going?', implying that I

Nine years on, they still look happy, although they appear to have shrunk a bit ...

165

Above: Graham in his 'I hear he's dug another hole' mode.

Opposite: Are these the real Lara Crofts? Katie Hirst, Kate Edwards and Jenni look butch for the cameras.

was making a different programme from his, etc. He and I have known each other for more than ten years, and he is one of my longest serving and most trusted directors, but that doesn't mean we always agree. After a certain amount of jovial (and not so jovial) banter things settled down and Graham agreed that he would cover Trench One retrospectively when he finally returned to the Gear site at 11.30 that morning. There was a bit of his usual good grace in this, which I appreciated, and harmony returned.

John Gater's first geophysics plot was a fantastic source of relief to me. The magnetometry showed archaeology and distinctive circular structures that could be Iron Age round houses. After consulting with Ian Powlesland and Pete Herring we agreed to put Trench One in over the part of a target that appeared on the geophysics as a circle with a blob in the centre of it. On Iron Age sites this is usually a round house with a hearth in the middle. The ideal with results like these would be to place a trench that covered both the

central feature and the exterior circle which might turn out to be either a ditch or a wall.

Magnetometry measures differences in magnetic strength. If a ditch is dug for the foundations of a house or to create a drain or pit it will eventually be filled with material that has a different magnetic signal to the original surface. It is fascinating stuff, and at the heart of the way it functions is the idea of coherence. The more the magnetic particles are lined up in the same direction, the more magnetic they will be. If a fire is lit on the floor of a prehistoric hut the original magnetic signal is removed and all the particles reset themselves to the current magnetic orientation of the earth's magnetic field. This fluctuates and changes slightly, and has occasionally reversed in the past, but any activity that disturbs the natural bedrock will subtly change the magnetic signal.

At the start of a survey the geophysics team have to set or calibrate their equipment so that it approximates the background magnetic signal of an undisturbed area. Any activity will be either more or less magnetic than this signal and will appear as a variation which produces a blob – whether this variation is positive or negative will depend on the coherence of the particles.

A large range of prehistoric pottery was appearing at the Caer Vallack site.

Fires, hearths, kilns and ditches containing slag or metalworking will give more coherent, and therefore stronger, magnetic signals – what John calls a 'strong positive'. When the blotchy version of a printout is turned into a spiky form the highly magnetic features turn into jagged spikes or, occasionally, a single huge spike – a 'Salisbury Cathedral' in *Time Team*'s shorthand description. At Gear Farm we had a wide range of variations: areas of lower coherence in the ditches of round houses and higher coherence on the hearths or burnt areas in their centres.

The other element I was glad to find out more about was the 'stagger filter'. It sounds like something that compensates for the previous night's drinking, but its real meaning helped me to understand why John, Chris Gaffney, Fiona Robertson and Christina Ruiz appeared to be loping along at such a regular pace when they were surveying the site.

Data is collected by walking along lines on a grid. A hearth in the middle of the grid will be transected by a number of passes by the surveyor. If he or she passes through it after twenty paces on line one, and then speeds up on line two and hits the hearth at twenty-one paces, or slows down and reaches

The length of Phil's thumbnail is due to his ambition to one day play the guitar.

it at nineteen and a half paces, the signal on the magnetometer will appear to come from a slightly earlier or later point on the ground. At the start of a geophysics survey surveyors can set their machines to beep at specific intervals so that they know that they should reach the end of the line within twenty 'beeps'. This is the familiar noise you may have heard in the background of *Time Team* geophysics sequences. If a whole set of passes is at differing speeds, or the operator is suffering from a hangover of momentous proportions, the passes will cross point X at slightly different times.

The 'stagger filter' is a nifty device that averages out the variations and brings the anomaly into line, making it clearer. Tony had a chance to give geophysics a go on this programme and saw for himself how difficult magnetometry is. He managed to combine a variable speed with a total lack of direction, and produced a survey line of limited straightness and irregular speed – what in geophysics terms might be called a 'staggered banana'.

What was apparent from John's results was that Gear Farm was providing very clear geophysics – a real bonus. It also became apparent that the geophysics team would have their work cut out to cover the whole site. Not only was it 7 hectares (18 acres) in size but our first scans had located complicated and excellent results that would require processing.

With Jenni on the ditch sectioning at Gear Farm, Katie Hirst looked after the trench in the round house there, which was to prove more exciting day by day. Meanwhile Barney Sloane was looking at the ditch and embankment at Caer Vallack and Carenza was investigating the centre of the settlement area there.

The geophysics survey at Gear Farm had first covered the area Rex had ploughed up to try his new crop. This was an important element in our strategy in that we would, possibly for the first time in Cornwall, have a concentrated area of archaeology that had been fieldwalked, metal detected, excavated and 'geofizzed'. The chance to do this kind of comparative archaeology is rare, and would give a fantastic set of data for the future. From the start of the project I'd felt that it was important to get good environmental evidence by sampling ditch fills and other deposits. Dr Vanessa Straker, an environmental archaeologist from Bristol University, was on hand to oversee any material taken from deep down in the trenches and I was hoping that once she'd had a chance to look at the samples more closely she would be able to build up a picture of the kind of crops that had been grown there and when they had been grown.

It was clear that Gear Farm had been occupied for thousands of years. Thanks to Rex's care in picking up everything he noticed, we had a range of finds from Neolithic flints through to late Iron Age pottery. In the past Rex had found medieval evidence, including a priest's ring, and we had a spur from the Civil War. Looking over the geophysics later that evening in the hotel it became apparent that there were underlying field systems that might even be Bronze Age. This made it important that the whole site, and not just the ploughed area, should be surveyed by the geophysics team – who were looking exhausted after just one day!

Towards the end of the Day One Barney had begun to find evidence that the ditch at Caer Vallack was huge and that it appeared to be cut into the rock. Were we dealing with a medieval structure, as Stewart Ainsworth had suggested earlier? Had a prehistoric round been reused during a later period?

Carenza's trench on some geophysics anomalies which looked like a settlement in the centre of Caer Vallack had begun to yield Iron Age pottery. This was evidence of occupation during that period, but would we find round houses? The interior of Caer Vallack had been landscaped by the Trelowarren Estate, the previous owners, and we knew that the oak trees on the rampart had been planted to beautify the area as a picnic spot. All this would confuse

Below: The depth of the ditch at Caer Vallack can clearly be seen.

Above: The team were joined by Peter Reynolds from Butser Ancient Village. All were clearly impressed by the size of Phil's bar bill!

Opposite: However many theories are suggested for a site, the answer is usually provided by grotty bits of prehistoric pottery like these.

the earlier archaeology. The ramparts and entrances of Iron Age sites are very important. They often had wooden palisades or revetments – wooden posts to strengthen or heighten the walls. When we look at any Iron Age site today we have to imagine them as much higher with complicated wooden structures on the top of the ramparts and at the entrances which act as doorways. These wooden posts at the entrance-ways can prove useful archaeologically because if you can find the post holes that remain, the material in them can help the site to be dated.

Back at Gear Farm, one of the two most important observations made at the beginning of Day Two was that the way the top of the hill sloped might have led to a build-up of soil that would have protected the archaeology lower down. Later that day I asked John to extend his grid down the hill to see if this was the case. The second was that Stewart confirmed that earthworks going up through the woods and connecting with crop marks we'd seen in aerial

photographs of the site meant that a major entrance must have connected Gear to a small inlet to the west, upstream of the River Helford. Had there originally been a small quay or port here? We knew that entrances are key locations, and that terminals – the ends of ditches – are often marked by ritually placed deposits, and so we decided to widen the trench.

We were now joined by our 1.8 metre (6 foot) Celt, Dave Freeman, who was going to demonstrate the weapon of choice for the average Iron Age warrior: the slingshot. I had always been fascinated by this apparently primitive weapon which, in the right hands, could be formidable. Sir Mortimer Wheeler had found hundreds of slingshot stones at Maiden Castle in Dorset. There had been a rumour that he'd brought in a few more from the beach to sell to visitors in order to sponsor the archaeology – but it was clear that any Iron Age site might well have a store of these stones.

Ella Galinski, who produces the cameos, had arranged for Dave to teach Phil how to use the slingshot (see pages 182–183). Rex was on hand with a radar gun – it took him a while to master its technology – as Dave lumbered up and sent stones whipping across the field. The gun told us that he was hitting around 60 mph and the sound the stones made as they flew through the air made you realise what a formidable weapon a slingshot could be. Members of opposing armies would have faced hundreds of them, and a single stone could clearly cause severe damage to a human being – even at 50 metres (55 yards).

By now fieldwalking had been completed over the ploughed areas and we also had results from the scans by the metal detectors. This showed how detectors working within a grid and alongside archaeologists are an invaluable part of an exercise like our work at Gear Farm. We all hoped this would show how they should work on other sites. Each of their finds could be precisely located – and it is often the exact position of an object that is important to understanding a site.

Towards the end of Day Two we opened up the area of the entrance. Jamie Wiggins, the unit manager and his team of runners went to work with their bowsaws and we cleared the scrub and began peeling back the topsoil. We were joined at the entrance-way by Jackie Nowakowski, an archaeologist who has dug many major Iron Age sites in Cornwall. Her advice was invaluable in positioning the trench at the entrance-way and with Ian's OK we decided to widen it to include more of the terminal. The pottery that was still coming out of the trenches in the interior implied that the main period of activity on the

site had been during the Iron Age, and by the end of the day we had placed another trench in a double-ditch feature that might just be a barrow. At Caer Vallack Carenza had found more Iron Age pottery and a piece of polished axe – probably Neolithic in date.

Day Three, Mick and I were keen to see the results of John's 'down the hill' survey. These duly appeared at 11.00 and they were, if anything, better than the geophysics results from Day One and Day Two, in that they were stronger, less broken and there appeared to be more detail and cleaner lines. Did this mean that the archaeology was better preserved? With only seven hours left we had to get a trench in immediately.

At this stage I issued the usual Day Three worry to Graham – that the archaeology had to go ahead at its own speed and he'd have to catch up if a camera wasn't on hand. For directors, Day Three is the final opportunity to clear up the odds and ends of scenes that help to tell the story, but anything that is started archaeologically has to be finished so we have to maximise our time in the trenches. All hands to the pump, and away we went on the final trenches in the lower part of the field. On Day Three no machines or excavators are allowed to stop digging unless Mick or I tell them to. On a previous programme someone had stopped working without my permission, and my reaction on that occasion meant it hadn't happened again! The sound quality is so good on *Time Team* that the crews occasionally ask a digger to stop working so that they can get the best possible sound. This can't happen on Day Three, the archaeology has to take priority and the crews have to hang on and do the best job they can in the circumstances. The majority of sites produce the best archaeology in the final hours of a shoot and if digging stops, for whatever reason, this may not happen.

The mass of archaeology coming out of both sites meant there was bound to be a time when we had to cut our cloth to meet the time available. I felt that we needed to have one more trench at Caer Vallack to try and solve the occupation question, and the obvious place to put it was the entrance-way. I'd been fighting for the archaeology in the morning and I now needed to

Rex Hosking, Ian Morrison and Mick discuss the future management of the site.

push it a bit further in the afternoon. The idea of looking for archaeology in the entrance-way was a good one – but the time had become tight. After a chat with Mick we both went to see Ian to argue our case.

Ian was sympathetic, but felt that because of the difficulty of interpreting the entrance way archaeology – it was likely to be complex and multilayered – we wouldn't have time to complete the job properly. Both Mick and I agreed with him, but I asked for a last geophysics survey to see if Barney's big ditch could be located running across the entrance. This meant another target for John, but once again he rose to the challenge and a survey began.

At Gear Farm, the trench on the lower slopes of the hill had begun to produce some amazing archaeology. It looked as though we had not one but two ditches around a central burnt area that was peppered with fragments of Iron Age pottery, some of which was black burnished ware of a high quality which was decorated with a pattern that looked as if it had been applied with a small comb.

I knew that Phil Harding and Tony had to get in a car at 6.00 to begin a journey to Gatwick and a meeting with dinosaurs and rattlesnakes in the USA

Pieces of flint like this indicated the site had been occupied for thousands of years before the Romano-British period.

for a *Time Team* documentary. We had an hour left and I was was watching the sectioning of the ditch by Kerry and Trevor, our diggers. Suddenly Kerry came up with a big grin and waved a piece of terracotta pot at me. 'My God,' said Ian when we showed it to him. It was a piece of an amphora – a storage jar – proof that our Iron Age ancestors at Gear had had access to high-status imports like wine and olive oil. Here was a wonderful final piece in the puzzle: evidence of contact with another culture and of the status of our settlement.

Had the jar come up the River Helford on an Iron Age boat that had perhaps made contact with a Mediterranean vessel or, more likely, a trader from France who had carried the amphora across the Channel? We could tell from the curve of the shape, and the size of the terracotta piece, that the jar would have been large and probably one of many that were brought to Gear and which contained luxury goods befitting the status of this Iron Age 'city'. At an early stage of the Gear Farm project I had read an article by my

Opposite: Finds like this, along with the piece of amphora, opened up a whole new aspect of Gear's history.

Above: Local volunteers watch as Tony and Carenza look at the finds from Caer Vallack.

favourite historian on Cornwall, Charles Henderson, who had referred to the possibility that Gear might have been a prehistoric 'city' – less a technical term than implying there were a lot of people there. It was very nice for me to think that we'd been able to confirm his intuition. The evidence from the geophysics surveys indicated that there may have been twenty or thirty Iron Age houses here.

The final puzzle was Caer Vallack, which might turn out to be a new kind of Iron Age monument. Could it be one of such high status that the tribe who owned it made the effort to cut the huge ditch into the rock that surrounded it that we had found?

It was amazing, as we finally sent Phil and Tony on their way, to reflect on how three days of work had opened a completely new chapter on the Iron Age in Cornwall. The mass of Iron Age structures surrounded by such an important earthwork combined with the fieldwalking and excavation finds, is probably unique, archaeologically, on such a site in Cornwall. It was good to think that all this had started because one Cornish farmer had taken the care to pick up some interesting bits and pieces on the surface of his fields.

Opposite: Trying to draw together some final conclusions. The tall chap in the centre is Ian Morrison, English Heritage inspector, who made an invaluable contribution to the success of the dig.

Below: Heading towards the final piece to camera, just out of screen, cars were waiting to whisk Tony and Phil off to America.

ELLA'S CAMEO:
IRON AGE SLINGS AND ROUND HOUSES

One Celt, one slingshot. Imagine facing 200 of them, all similarly armed – a frightening prospect!

With two fascinating Iron Age sites to investigate in Cornwall, we decided to keep the cameo sequences to a minimum. We took Phil to visit a wonderful round house, newly constructed with granite walls and thatch by Fred Musty in Bodrifty – an amazing place very near to Penzance, complete with a whole village of ruined ancient round houses. We also made an Iron Age sling. It seemed appropriate to do this as we knew that slingshot stones had been collected from the site at Gear.

Dave Freeman, an imposing giant of a man in full Celtic costume, joined us for the demonstration and the first thing he did was show Phil how to create a sling in a matter of minutes. Making it was remarkably simple. All that was needed was a small rectangle of leather, gathered at the corners to create a shallow pouch; two leather thongs; and some round beach pebbles. It was amazing that such basic components could create a weapon that was capable of killing.

They were now ready to test the sling. I knew that Dave was very experienced with one – but could Phil pick up the technique quickly, and would our camera be capable of capturing the speed and power of the tiny stone? The first challenge was to get Phil into action. It turned out that it was crucial to release one of the thongs connected to the pouch at precisely the right moment during the swing – otherwise the stone might be flung backwards instead of forwards. True to form, Phil managed to get the hang of how the sling worked extremely quickly. However, the throw he used was an underarm one – the easiest – and the speed and distance weren't too impressive.

At an early stage we'd decided that we wanted to know just how fast a stone could travel. Speed on impact would equal potential killing power. So I'd hired a small radar gun normally used to measure tennis serves. We brought in Rex to operate it and set up some trial runs. It was really funny because operating the camera turned out to be a lot more difficult than using the sling. A succession of stones were slung and we managed to capture the speed of Phil's arm, passing birds and a stationary hedge – anything other than the projectile! Phil lamented the fact that speed cameras on the road don't seem to have the same problems when you drive past them too fast.

All this practice served to increase Phil and Dave's expertise and they were eventually reaching speeds in the region of 70 mph with the underarm throw. (I have to admit, though, that we were never quite sure whether the radar gun was recording the speed of the arm movement or the tiny stone's flight.)

The sling was perhaps one of man's first powerful long-distance weapons – and one of the lowest tech ones. It was clear that at a distance of 20 to 30 metres (22 to 33 yards) it could have been lethal. We had hoped to show the damage by targeting a watermelon, but Dave persuaded us that the sling was generally used against hoards of attackers and that accuracy wasn't its main attribute (so much for the David and Goliath story), so we didn't waste time trying this.

One interesting fact was that the sling was definitely respected and feared by the Romans when they were attacking Britain. They even carried special tweezers in their medical kit to extract stones embedded in muscle. An attack on Gear would have been a very serious proposition if the defenders had been armed with slings.

Phil back in the Iron Age, complete with hut and Celtic home-owners.

Conclusion

2001 saw the *Time Team* production system put under pressure from the start by the foot-and-mouth outbreak, and I was delighted that everyone pulled together to make the series a success.

Each of the six programmes described in this book created specific challenges and faced us with unique archaeological problems. As usual, we had to start with a potential hypothesis and keep testing it by excavation. *Time Team*, I believe, is still unique in the way it tries to resolve and answer questions by excavating sites in front of the cameras. The questions are not of the high-flying theoretical variety. They are down-to-earth and can only be answered by incontrovertible evidence rigorously examined by the team and Tony. Questioning the experts – pushing them to explain their ideas concisely and to be clear about the basis for their conclusions – has been part of *Time Team*'s attitude from the start.

At Vauxhall, the issue of whether or not we had a pit or a post hole was finally resolved by a small section of the trench close to the post – physical evidence worth more than any number of theories. At High Ercall, the idea that a southern wall had once taken the brunt of a Civil War attack was only proved in the last hour by finding its foundations in the trench. The evidence is often small and ephemeral, but it is essential that it can stand up to scientific analysis. At Gear, a single piece of an amphora – no more than 3–4 centimetres (1– 1½ inches) long – suddenly opened up a connection with the Mediterranean world of olives and wine. Because it was found in a well-dug trench that gave it a context and a secure location in the stratigraphy, it can form the basis for a whole new set of ideas about Gear. We now know that the people who lived there had contact with traders who were possibly operating from the coast of France.

When you see diggers toiling away on *Time Team*, with an air of concentrated effort, they are making sure the trenches are being dug correctly. Only this allows us to be certain about our conclusions. Care and accuracy are equally important in the process of recording and drawing the trenches, which takes place once excavation stops. This means that other archaeologists, perhaps some distance in the future, will be able to examine what we have done and draw their own conclusions. As we get asked to do increasingly important sites these records become essential. Each *Time Team* programme represents a unique contribution to the archaeological record: a total of nearly eighty or so sites which would not have been excavated otherwise – eighty insights into the past. Over the last two or three years we have benefitted from a fairly consistent team of diggers: Kerry Ely, Ian Powlesland, Barney Sloane, Katie Hirst and Jenni Butterworth. They have now been joined by Kate Edwards whose job it is to coordinate the recording of the trenches and the writing up of the final reports.

Alongside our ongoing determination to keep the archaeology up to scratch we have also been keen to develop our contacts with local archaeologists and other people who have begun to realise that *Time Team* can help them to answer questions that have been left unanswered for years. Of all the sites we excavated this year, it was particularly satisfying to do justice to the work of Jean Mullinger and her family. A lot of people are struggling to find out about their local area, putting in the effort to do so after they finish their day job, and it is they who bother to write and send ideas to us. It's great to feel that we can, in some programmes, recognise their efforts. We wouldn't have gone to Gear if Rex Hosking had not followed up his interest in what his fields were revealing; and it was the enthusiasm of an army officer that made Chicksands happen. At High Ercall the owner of the house was prepared to pursue the history of his home, and it's good to think that this kind of interest can make it through to become a programme.

We've given a bit more space to cameos in this book than we have in previous ones, and I hope you've enjoyed Ella's insights into them. They test theories to breaking point – the gun is fired, the charcoal-burners are pushed to their limits and, again, the cameras are there to see success and failure, the highs and lows of real experiments.

2001 has seen us producing *Time Team* documentaries that enable us to follow sites in more detail than the three-day format allows – our experiences over the last ten years have given us confidence to face new and more complex sites. Both the *Time Team* shoots, and the documentaries, have increasingly included Scheduled Ancient Monuments and sites of international importance, like our work at Hadrian's Wall.

This year we tackled two sites that are examples of this. One of these, potentially the location of a ship that was wrecked after the Armada was defeated, involved a three-day dive off the coast of Scotland. With Phil, Carenza, Tony and Katie Hirst all using their diving skills, we were amazed to discover a fantastic collection of Italian Renaissance pottery – a present or bribe

from a Spanish lord to an English ally. The logistical challenges of this site created a team of people who have now gone on to look at one of Nelson's ships which was wrecked off the Scilly Isles. Again, our work involved establishing good working relationships with the key archaeologists – in this case the Archaeological Diving Unit led by Martin Dean – and the enthusiasts who made the discovery in the first place.

This year's live programme on a potential Saxon cemetery produced not only amazing finds but also a set of mysteries which it will take some time to solve. It is part of *Time Team*'s commitment to the archaeology that we will be funding post-excavation costs on the artefacts, which included a unique set of Anglo-Saxon buckets. We will also support research work into the site, which may well turn out to be one of the most important cemeteries excavated in recent times.

Sites like these are beginning to make a significant difference to our view of the past. *Time Team* is rescuing unique information and placing it in the archaeological record. I hope this book has given you an insight into what goes on behind the scenes. The new series will be broadcast from January 2002 and Jenni and I have already begun to look at new ideas for Series Ten. I hope you continue to enjoy the programmes, and continue to join us in the ongoing adventure of *Time Team*.

In this traumatic year of foot-and-mouth, a final thought about the farmers. Archaeologists, their bosses and the government need to realise that farmers are often the first line of contact with the archaeology. Supported and encouraged, they are a fantastic resource – people who can discover new material and are in the best position to care for it. A policy that helps them to do this, and that makes members of the farming community feel that an archaeological find on their land is a positive event, is essential. Promotion of a policy that recognises their need both to make a living and preserve the past could lead to a more positive use of what is a major resource for archaeologists: the eyes, good sense and awareness of Britain's farmers.

Opposite: This burial was just one of many graves we found near Salisbury on this year's Live. The strange appearance of the two skeltons apparently buried face to face left a strong and lasting impression on all of us.

Above: Phil looking at the first pieces of pottery brought up from what may prove to be a Spanish Armada wreck.

INDEX

ACKNOWLEDGEMENTS

I am indebted to a number of individuals who have helped with the compilation of material for this book, especially Jackie Stinchcombe, Ella Galinski, Nick Corcos and Jenni Butterworth. Many thanks to Victor Ambrus for his illustrations.

Many people worked on the programmes featured in this book, and I would like to thank the directors: Michael Douglas, Graham Dixon, Patrick McGrady and Laurence Vulliamy; the assistant producers: Ella Galinski and Sarah Walmsley; the researchers: George Pagliero, Ishbel Macdonald, Jenni Butterworth and Ben Dempsey; and the production team: Zarina Dick, Karla Goodman, Melinda Smith and Jamie Wiggins.

Many thanks also to our own digging and survey teams and to all the archaeologists who worked so hard on these sites with us, especially: Gustav Milne, Jon Cotton and all at the Museum of London Archaeology Service, Francis Pryor, Richard Morriss, Roberta Gilchrist, Paul Belford and Ironbridge Archaeology, Glenn Foard, Guy de la Bédoyère, Margaret Cox, Henrietta Quinnell, Peter Herring and the Cornwall Archaeological Unit, and Ian Morrison and John Ette of English Heritage.

Final thanks must go to the people who inspired us with their enthusiasm for these special sites: Jean Mullinger and family; Rex, Pat and Andrew Hosking; and all the staff at Chicksands.

TIME TEAM
COLLECTION

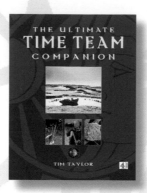

FOR THE ULTIMATE TIME TEAM COMPANION:

Tim Taylor draws on the expertise of the **Time Team** contributors to answer all your questions about the programme, including a guide to fifty excavation sites illustrating our history from the dawn of time to the modern age. Available now priced £12.99.

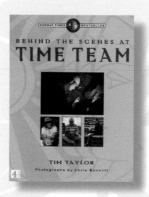

FOR TIME TEAM'S TIMECHESTER:

Time Team's Timechester: A Family Guide to Archaeology is an imaginatively created book which has a dual purpose: it is a history of British settlement and an introduction to archaeological methods. Available now priced £16.99.

FOR BEHIND THE SCENES AT TIME TEAM:

Behind the Scenes at Time Team looks at the work that goes in to making the series: how the sites are chosen, what life is like during the three-day digs, and the most exciting finds. Available now priced £12.99.

All available directly from the Channel 4 Shop.
Please phone 0870 744 44 44 or write to The Channel 4 Shop, 33 Park Royal Road, London, NW10 7LN